Daphne and the Centaurs – Overcoming Gender Based Violence

This publication has been produced with the financial support of the DAPHNE III Programme of the European Union for the Project 'EMPoWER: Empowerment of Women – Environment Research'. The contents of this publication are the sole responsibility of the authors of each contribution (article/chapter) and can in no way be taken to reflect the views of the European Commission.

The publication is published thanks to the Department of Philosophy, Sociology, Pedagogy and Applied Psychology (FISPPA) of the University of Padova, and is also edited under the auspices of GDG – Forum on Gender Differences and Inequalities, Italian Association of Psychology; CIRSG – Centre on Italian Gender Research and Studies of the University of Padova.

Caterina Arcidiacono
Ines Testoni
Angelika Groterath (eds.)

Daphne and the Centaurs – Overcoming Gender Based Violence

Barbara Budrich Publishers
Opladen • Berlin • Toronto 2013

A CIP catalogue record for this book is available from
Die Deutsche Bibliothek (The German Library)

© 2013 by Barbara Budrich Publishers, Opladen, Berlin & Toronto
www.barbara-budrich.net

ISBN   978-3-8474-0124-7 (paperback)
eISBN   978-3-8474-0492-7 (e-book)

Die Deutsche Bibliothek – CIP-Einheitsaufnahme
Ein Titeldatensatz für die Publikation ist bei Der Deutschen Bibliothek erhältlich.

Verlag Barbara Budrich 🅑 Barbara Budrich Publishers
Stauffenbergstr. 7. D-51379 Leverkusen Opladen, Germany

86 Delma Drive. Toronto, ON M8W 4P6 Canada
www.barbara-budrich.net

Jacket illustration by Bettina Lehfeldt, Kleinmachnow, Germany –
www.lehfeldtgraphic.de
Language editing: Máiréad Collins, Belfast, UK
Typesetting: Petra Reiners, Bonn, Germany – www.buchfinken.com
Printed in Europe on acid-free paper by
paper&tinta, Warsaw

Content

Part 3. Strategies and tools

Foreword

Ines Testoni, Caterina Arcidiacono, Angelika Groterath

"Daphne and the centaurs: Overcoming gender based violence" originated as a response to a fundamental question about the roots of gender-based violence and how to fight it. In this sense, it offers a systematic reflection on femicide's socio-cultural roots as well as the goals and effects of concrete actions and their psychological tools they bring to practice.

The mythological and cultural anthropological key that thematizes the volume traces the history of violence against women instituted within a framework of apparent affection: brutality within the region of love. It talks about the cultural origin of gender violence and female victimization, despite the great efforts of the Western world to resolve the gender gap. In fact, the problem in many European Countries has remained unchanged for decades and, despite the significant number of European policies promoted to solve it, nothing seems to be able to reduce the persistent submission of women to traditional colonialist logics that keep them strongly subordinate to men, especially in Southern areas.

This volume considers the context of several cultural frames characterizing the multiple backgrounds of Europe, which, in some cases, have held back the emancipation of women, or at least have maintained the backlash against feminism. It is composed of three parts: the first discusses some theoretical questions inherent to the roots of male violence and the culture of victimization of women; the second presents some practical interventions in the field of treatment for the consequences of male violence and in the field of prevention; the third discusses some useful tools for research in this area. Indeed the whole volume is focused on the instruments, which may result in effectively changing this situation, considering both sociological and psycho-social aspects involved.

In the first chapter of the first section, "Why is Antigone still alive? Despite spitting on Hegel and Freud, the tragic Italian women's contemporary situation", Ines Testoni discusses what is happening in European Countries and especially in Italy, where the female condition is in a particularly critical situation. Testoni's analysis of the Italian condition in this piece is useful as it can be considered as being similar or prototypic to Latin cultures, such as Spanish, Portuguese, or Southern ones. It is important to remind the reader that, during the 20th session of the UN Human Rights Council, on 25 June 2012, the Special Rapporteur on *"Violence against women, its causes and consequences"*, Rashida Manjoo, opened the session with an important report denouncing gender violence in Italy. She stressed that weak political will and the lack of funds for activities in the area of women's rights are causes and effects of a cultural backwardness that maintains female subjugation[1]. In Italy, and we suppose also in Southern Europe, the revolutionary theories of the Second and Third Feminist Waves are not widely known, and are discussed only in selected women's groups and within an academic gender studies environment, and this situation does not seem to develop in parallel with women's ability to enjoy the benefits of change. The feminist culture gives the impression of being unable to involve the masses of young women and of being intrinsically powerless to indicate solutions for the serious discrimination that women experience. In this chapter, Ines Testoni indicates some key concepts which can show how the levers of female emancipation are disabled by cultural processes.

Following this cultural discussion, in the second chapter Luigi Zoja presents *"Centaurs. A violent masculine myth"*, which considers the mythological roots of the exercise of male violence against women. In modern law and custom, gang rape has always been considered a crime, whereas in past ages it was a tolerated exception. This chapter's investigation of the mythical, historical, biological and cultural antecedents of the masculine impulse to rape goes beyond individual pathology. It aims to analyse *collective rape* and the potential model of uncritical behaviour that it embodies. One would expect gang rape to be an increasingly rare occurrence. But in fact it returned in an uncontrolled form in the Second World War, and since then seems to have become a recurrent epidemic on the margins of the former colonies of western nations. The importance of this chapter is both concrete and symbolic. Indeed we can consider violence as a cusp characterizing gender based violence, but also as a specific expression of male strategies used to victimize women in all the expression of their intimate and social life. In this sense it is important to recognize the cultural basis of this phenomenon. Just as with the centaur, where there was no difference between sexual life and sexual violence and in his eyes rape was the only true form of sexuality; to some men there is no difference between subjugation of women and practice of legitimate power. Nor is there any distinction between war and orgiastic violence against women from the perspective of centaurs or the men in question; hence today this perverse ecstasy may be termed *centaurism*.

---

1   See: Wideplus, 2013: http://wideplusnetwork.wordpress.com/news/un-special-rapporteur-on-feminicide-and-violence-against-women-in-italy/

After Luigi Zoja's dramatic description, the following chapter by Claudio Tugnoli titled "*The Goddess Culture: Gylanic Model versus Androcratic Model*" resumes the discussion on the mythological construction of the victimary position of women, through the literature of famous texts from Gimbutas. Archeological findings have supported the hypothesis that a notable cultural turnover in Europe and in the Near East was caused by the invasion of hordes of pastoral nomads known under the name of "Kurgan". The Kurgan invasions caused deep-set upheavals and radical changes in what was Europe at that time: its civilization was suddenly interrupted and destroyed at the edge of the 5th and the 4th millennium B.C. The inhabitants of Old Europe were sedentary horticulturists who lived in unfortified and unarmed dwelling clusters. Their civilization was egalitarian, matrilineal and matrilocal and overall essentially peaceful. Conversely, the Kurgan were herdsmen whose society was based on a patrilineal organization. They lived in small seasonal settlements and reared their animals on a free range basis. The divide between the old Europeans and the Kurgan was evident, not only in family life and in material conditions, but also in their beliefs. While the Europeans envisaged a Creative Mother as the personification of the feminine principle that represented the agricultural cycle of birth, death and regeneration, the Kurgan on the contrary upheld heroes and warrior gods, divinities that supported lighting and thunder. Within this fulcrum Claudio Tugnoli places the beginning of gender-based violence against women.

The theme of victimization is furthermore discussed by Marco Monzani, in "*Awareness of victimization and request for help: Two moments of the same path*", where he considers the difficulties faced by female victims to recognize their condition and their rights. The author discusses the thought of Emilio Viano, teacher of criminology and victimology at the University of Washington and director of the International magazine Victimology, who defines the victim of an abuse as any subject injured or that has suffered wrongdoing on the part of others, who perceives herself to be a victim, who shares the experience with others looking for help, assistance and compensation, who is recognized as a victim and who presumably is being helped by public, private or collective agencies/structures. Marco Monzani goes on to define a further dimension, outlining the difficult requirement that victims become aware of their victimary condition, where the cultural frame prevents it, since this educates the same woman to believe that male violence is the correction expression of a man's strength.

The second part, examining some good practices, presents the analysis of clinical and legal cases in order to better explain the complexity of the variables involved in the elaboration of violence, from the individual dimension to the symbolic-cultural and political-legislative ones. Caterina Arcidiacono's chapter highlights how prescriptions and gender role representations impact on policy relating to social and juridical services facing domestic violence.

"Women as mothers, lovers, and wives" discusses the representation of role-based violence presenting a case-story of a couple gender violence and its implications for motherhood definitions. If the value attributed to parental care varies across diverse historical periods, what is the vision that must orientate a health worker? What is the best form of motherhood? Might it be the natural mother bond? Is the maternal or the paternal rule to be in force? These questions underpin the placing and replacing of children in difficulty in different contexts. These questions cannot be implicit but are matters of which we must be explicitly aware, especially when we have a mother that in her role of woman and lover is subjected to intimate violence.

In the chapter *"From the maternal to the Self: psychodrama for the promotion of female agency in overcoming the internalized victimary role"*, Ines Testoni and collaborators, through qualitative research, analyze the maternal role in an empowering project. The authors consider the problem of motherhood's psychological role with respect to their daughters that are victims of domestic violence. In particular it shows how mothers are seen by their daughters as unable to teach them to deal with the problem and unable to give them the necessary support. The authors, assuming the gender perspective, believe that this problem is determined by cultural causes, which prevent women from creating genuine relationships of solidarity and mutual understanding.

In the following chapter "You made your bed, now you can lie in it: the biodynamic understanding of healing the social mechanisms keeping women in abusive relationships", Denise Saint Arnaud and collaborators describe the female empowering processes from the Biodynamic Psychology (BP) point of view. They argue that social and cultural rules can be transmitted across generations unconsciously, in the form of an energetic and emotional charge. Their position considers that such a charge is carried within the cells and tissues of the individuals of the community, since individual cells may be bathed in these fears and constraints since before the individual's birth, making the prospect of being freed from them seem impossible. Therefore, assuming BP point of view, which theorizes that social change, as well as individual health, occurs at the cellular level, the authors link the social change with the cellular change, and provide examples from Biodynamic intervention designed to facilitate healing from domestic and sexual abuse.

Another psychotherapeutic perspective is assumed by Leandra Perrotta who, starting from the Jungian point of view, considers the *"Transgenerational echoes of violence: Jungian Psychodrama as a path to individuation"*. Social networks can both give support, as well as create social constraints towards helping people leave abusive relationships and enable healthy autonomy. These cultural mores and expectations are unspoken, ubiquitous, and "normal" for the person within her environment. While the person may consciously recognize them as a source of pain and constraint, they are often at a loss as to *how* to challenge them. Moreover, the community continues to operate by these fears and rules, making spontaneous free choice seem unattainable. In a community where gender based violence is unconsciously accepted and sustained by cultural frames, the victim-perpetrator relationship may often be the result of a mutual dependency that makes it difficult to break the vicious circle. In these cases Jungian Psychodrama can be a powerful psychological tool to allow women who are victims of violence to free themselves from dependence on the perpetrator, following the path toward individuation, which is a key concept of Jungian outlook. Leandra Perrotta describes this route through the analysis of some specific problems and their resolutions.

The third part showcases the results of preventive and therapeutic interventions, developed within European and international projects, aimed to establish a large European study of intervention on gender based violence against women and to evaluate the effectiveness of different methods.

Giuseppe Stanziano and Adele Nunziante Cesaro present the research *"Thinking, feeling, acting: the T.A.T. in brief psychological consultation with women victims of violence"*, whose technique is specific for the study of violence further elaborating the research tool proposed by the French psychoanalyst Chaterine Chabert.,

Mihaela Bucuta and Gabriela Dima, in their chapter *"The experience of domestic violence: an interpretative-phenomenological analysis*, present the Interpretative Phenomenological Analysis (IPA) as a meaningful tool to deepening the analysis of thoughts, feelings and behaviors of women submitted to marital violence. In the last contribution *"Empowering female victims of domestic violence: the measure of effectiveness between spontaneity and wellbeing"*, Ines Testoni and collaborators present the validation of the assessment of the *Empower project* and the efficacy of its psychodramatic intervention[2]. This intervention-research means to determine whether, after the psychodramatic treatment, there has been a change in the physical and psychological well-being and in the level of spontaneity and creativity shown by the participants.

The final aim of the volume is then to widen the debate on measures and tools that psychology and psychotherapeutic knowledge can offer to victims and perpetrators of violence in fighting abusive relationships.

---

2   *Empower* is a project that fits within the perspective of prevention and intervention in the context of domestic violence, ending the cycle of re-victimization of women. The European Partners in the project include the following countries: Italy (leader) Austria, Portugal, Bulgaria, Romania and Albania (external partner). Empower aims to establish a large European study of intervention on domestic violence against women. The objective of this research is to evaluate the effectiveness of the combined ecological and psychodrama methods.

Part 1. Theoretical aspects

Why is Antigone still alive?
Despite spitting on Hegel and Freud, the tragedy of the contemporary Italian woman's situation

Ines Testoni

Introduction

The European Women's Lobby (EWL) believes that the systematic exclusion of women from social and political power determines the phenomenon of multiple discrimination worldwide, so that within each social disadvantaged population the status of women is always the worst. Despite the great efforts of the Western world aimed at resolving this injustice, the gender gap in Italy has stood still for decades and is at unsustainable levels (ISTAT, 2011). Furthermore, even after the considerable efforts made by European policies, which Italy adheres to in order to reduce this injustice, nothing seems to be able to reduce the persistent humiliation of women by and their acquiescence to traditional logic keeping them strongly subordinate to men and therefore making incompatible the dimensions *de jure* and *de facto*.

Although women graduate from higher institutions in greater numbers than men, work in a variety of roles, and have expertise across the private and public realms, they have failed to improve their position consolidated from the 1980's to the present day (Alma Laurea, 2007). Since equal access to positions of higher status is an indicator of democracy and civilization, it is important to investigate what factors contribute in determining such an imbalance. Almost 20 years of the Berlusconi government has highlighted the absolute powerlessness of Italian women, with regard to self-preservation so that they still seem unable to reach at least the number indicated by Georg. W. F. Hegel in *Phänomenologie des Geistes* (*Phenomenology of spirit*) (1977) and which Karl Marx developed to mark a point of no return in the history of mankind: the master-slave dialectic that elects self-awareness as the basic tool for liberating the individual from reification.

Italy is an industrial powerhouse that boasts a remarkable number of thinkers, artists and scientists, and is always on the verge of reaching an exemplary position in culture and development. Unfortunately the *Bel Paese*'s "take off" is derailed by the logic of exploitation and slavery that belongs to outmoded models where the status of women is among the more serious failures.

But it was not always so, in the seventies Italy knew the strength of an internationally recognized radical feminism. Carla Lonzi was one of the main movers and shakers of this movement, and she is still considered one of the most important representatives of the Italian feminist second wave. She is famous for her feminist treatise "Sputiamo su hegel. La donna vaginale e donna clitoridea" ("Let's spit on Hegel. The vaginal woman and the clitoral one"). The importance of her input is still alive today and has recently been underlined in a conference (Conte, 2011) where gender studies experts studied her message, considered revolutionary in the current Italian situation. If we consider women's activism of the seventies and the successes since then achieved by women in the rest of the Western world, it seems that in the last twenty years Italy has slipped into a regressive anti-historical decline. However, since this situation is very similar to neighboring theocratic countries, it would be better to think about some basic aspects perhaps too soon taken for granted: the substantial inability of women to free themselves from ideologies that value them for maternal and familial affectivity, since this is the drift-risk in which the feminist and essentialist theory of sexual difference incurs. Our analysis of this exquisitely Italian evidence, inherent to a number of difficulties not fully overcome in feminist history, is inevitably limited but at the same time strategic. Indeed, we think that it is worthwhile to underline again the issues that democracy still has to insist on, with stronger determination both in Italy and in other countries that are in a similar situation. With this perspective, we want to define what has happened in the last few decades, when forced and/or exploitative (immigrant) prostitution has guaranteed more and more profitable gains for the national and inter-national mafias on Italian roads, when the Italian television has celebrated women only within the categories of stupid, boring and trite sexual-things, when parliament is filled with escorts and sexy showgirls while keeping the percentage of women in politics equal to that of the seventies, where female employment is unstoppably slipping down, where motherhood is celebrated as sacred while artificial insemination and assisted reproductive technologies are prohibited, and yet no social structure exists to help mothers in their daily care of children. A country in which the number of femicides is increasing faster than any other European country, so that almost every day a woman is murdered by her husband, boyfriend or ex-lover who could not accept the changing role that his partner is experiencing after years of subordination. All of this has been happening, while on the other hand, Italian academic gender studies have achieved increasing international success. In actual fact, third wave feminism opened wide horizons where the right to self-determination is open to everyone, but in fact this does not occur in reality, even in the Western world where these ideas were born and continue to develop. Italy is an excellent example of this, since feminist theory does not seem to provide a parallel ability for women to enjoy the benefits of historical change.

In Italy we think that the "cultural motherhood role" is crucial. Italy is a country of amoral familism (Banfield, 1958), where social relationships are developed under the matricentric law of blood ties and kinship, where the subsequent mafia style has severely contaminated the entire institutional activities, branching off into widespread lawlessness in which it is impossible to recognize any social pact and democratic foundation of a shared law (Testoni, 2007). Italy is also a country where catholic politics is tenaciously fighting against the self-determination of women, limiting the freedom of abortion, for example the "Mother" Church was able to influence the parliamentary decision to not allow the legalization of assisted reproductive technology and block any progress in granting the right to marriage for gay couples. Additionally, Italian feminism is still dominated by the sexual difference theory, which has significant collusive relationships with catholic new feminism (Testoni, 2012), founded on the essentialist perspective which emphasizes a belief in an integral complement between men and women, considering the female gender irreducibly different from the male one because of its fundamental predisposition to natural maternal procreation (Allen, 2006). Its main aim is to maintain women totally subordinate to the divine law manifested by nature and in this way to reject any imitation of a male model of social domination, acknowledging and affirming the true "genius of women" in every aspect of life in society (Benedict XVI, 2004; John Paul II, 1988, 1997).

This chapter tries to identify the possible internal strait of feminist thought, where the contraposition between catholic feminism and revolutionary feminism remains in the background, in order to recognize how the maternal dimension produces a block to an authentic emancipation of women, considering Italy not as a marginal region of Western culture but as a particularly significant place where the cusp between the two feminisms is most evident. We would first clarify that, as Italian women's situation is still far behind that of women living in Anglophone countries, we assume the crucial perspective of Gayatri Chakravorty Spivak (1999) with respect to genderism, accepting her idea of "strategic essentialism," or the "necessary error" which has to be performed consciously whenever it becomes vital to remove discrimination. Then, we emphasize the term "woman" not in order to adopt any essentialist perspective versus the post-gender one, but because we believe that the conventional use of such a concept, critically assumed not as an ontological category but as an existential condition, still needs to reflect on the causes of females acquiescence to subjugation.

The *fil rouge* we follow moves along a path that evidently is not yet concluded. In fact, it starts from the Hegelian master-slave dialectic to penetrate into the tragic figure of Antigone, which still represents the inability of the Italian woman to enter and pass such a dialectic.

Let's spit on Hegel: From Simone de Beauvoir to Carla Lonzi

In 1970 Carla Lonzi created, along with Carla Accardi and Elvira Banotti, a group-movement of female self-consciousness, whose first act was posting on the streets of Rome and Milan their founding "Manifesto di Rivolta Femminile" ("Manifesto of female Rebellion") (Lonzi, 1974) where the pride of female difference versus equality with man, the radical rejection of the complementarity of women with men, the institution of marriage, the recognition of women's work as productive work, the centrality of the body, the claim of a sexual self, independent of the needs and desires of men and the alliance and solidarity among women were declared and planned into future political action. Inside these female rebellion activity groups, women used their personal experiences to analyze the oppression and gender role conformity within the family as well as in the society they were victims of, in order to provide themselves with a new concept of their individual and social identity (Ravera, 1978; Scaraffia & Isastia, 2002). Indeed, the liberation aims of the second feminist wave were immersed in the Marxist-Freudian milieu, and the concept of the unconscious was key, therefore in order to make those assumptions feasible, it was necessary to know and show the drama of life and to recognize how internalized unconscious convictions, coming from an oppressive education, were still working inside. However, in the meantime it was inevitable to amend and deconstruct both the Marxist and the Freudian theory from sexist contamination, that resulted from a patriarchal and oppressive culture. In this sense, "the personal becomes political" aimed at eliminating subordination and destroying the prison in which they had been relegated: the bourgeois family. However, beginning with Hegel, neither Marx nor Freud could be uncritically accepted.

In *Let's spit on Hegel,* Carla Lonzi defines the cause that Marxism, as a concrete historical revolution from the Hegelian master-slave dialectic, has been a story of men, unable to emancipate women from their subjugation. In her viewpoint, Hegel's theory is sexist, and incapable of liberating females from male oppression because it considers women as a fundamental element of family, representing the "divine law."

Hegel has gained more and more importance as an issue in feminist critiques, starting from Simone de Beauvoir (1949), who in *The Second sex* articulates one of the central questions with which political feminists are concerned: the critique of the absolute which determines the crystallization of the desire for human beings to escape their freedom by submerging it into an external absolute, justifying the sacrifice of countless individuals. The dimension of religiosity and divinity belongs specifically to this area. The critique begins by attacking the structure of Hegelian thought, whose absolute, similarly to any religion, represents an abstraction which is taken as the truth of existence which, instead of signifying and valorizing, humiliates individual human lives. Despite her critique of Hegel, de Beauvoir does not deny the dialectic and does not relegate individual realization to a solipsistic dimension, but considers "otherness" essential for the construction of the self, in order to define oneself as an individual. Therefore, her analysis shows how women cannot access this process because they are objectified by men who offer them no reciprocity. Indeed women are consistently defined as the "other" by men, and as incidental and inessential, since man is the subject and woman is the "other," but not vice versa. As far as marriage is concerned, the nuclear family is the first area where women are relegated and the female construction of the Self becomes inessential.

As discussed by feminist critiques of Hegelian *Phenomenology of spirit* (Jagentowitz Mills, 1996), the "other" that women consist in is the "divine law" contrasting "human law," where the first is the unconscious nature of women and the second is the conscious construction of humankind's history and its liberation from the same nature. Certainly, Hegel references the feminine as that from which history begins but that is, in itself, an a-historical event, and the unconscious place in which women reign (in the family). Subsequently, the family institution is the intimate dimension based on "natural" relationships rooted in sentiment and feeling, which is the inverse of that found in society where participants see themselves as separate individuals having relationships with "otherness" as a self-conscious individual. Thus, men who meet each other in the "otherness" of social historical dimensions (labour and market spheres) need their subjectivity in these relationships, as they do in the family, where they are subject to opposed historical influences.

In this field, the contribution of Patricia Jagentowicz Mills (Jagentowitz Mills, 1996), is particularly important in terms of her analysis of the mythological figure of Antigone discussed in the *Phenomenology* by Hegel and is associated with primitive gods of nature as opposed to the more rational and masculine figure of Creon. The Hegelian perspective considers Antigone, and women more generally, linked to the archaic human condition, incapable of true spiritual agency or ethical behavior, respecting rational law. Recently, Kimberley Hutchings and Tuija Pulkkinen (2010) have collected state of the art feminist studies on Hegelian discrimination of women, and the common idea of all contributions is that which Carla Lonzi discussed in 1974, immediately after De Beauvoir: from the Hegelian perspective the modern bourgeois family definitely arose to become an ontologically unchangeable entity, which must be supported by women. Then, from de Beauvoir to Lonzi, feminists all over the world including Italy have become aware that this duty is alienating and keeps them in a dehumanizing condition: female lives restricted by domesticity are not fully human, and women who accept the socially-constructed belief in a divine will that pre-defines female nature and destiny are collusive with male strategies determining their enslavement. That is why Carla Lonzi used the exhortative metaphor "Let's spit on Hegel" to mobilize women to reach self-liberation from the Hegelian perspective, to leave their homes and get into the labour market and fully exploit all technological means available to ensure their full transcendence from the physical and cultural exigencies of conception, reproduction and family responsibilities. From this catchphrase, divorce and abortion were respectively legalized in 1974 and 1981, but since these remote conquests, in spite that university-educated women exceed men by 10 percent (and in the rest of Europe by two percent), currently only 45 percent of Italian women work outside the home, earning on average half the amount of their male counterparts and only seven percent occupying managerial positions. In the World Economic Forum's Global Gender Gap Report, Italy placed 80th, behind countries such as Botswana, Burundi, Jamaica, Kazakhstan, Kenya, Malawi, and Mozambique, and marking a four-point drop from 2009, furthermore placing Italy 89th in the Inter-Parliamentary Union's global classification of women in parliament (World Economic Forum, 2013). In this most catholic of countries, women still fail in relation to men, showing that they are unable to resist his claim to extensive and ubiquitous "complementary" satisfaction of his basic needs.

Let's spit on Freud: From Carla Lonzi to Julia Kristeva

The problem of the family intended by Hegel as an original and sacred place of social relationships has been discussed and widely refuted by Frederick Engels (1884), who defined it as not divine but originally matrilineal. This concept gradually evolved into state-building, and currently, into the bourgeois family, functioning to maintain "property" and the exploitative relationship between the upper classes and the socio-economically disadvantaged. On this trajectory, the ineffable and a-historical ground of the Hegelian female disposition to the natural dimension of the family, where women remain reclusive and satisfy corporal male and human-species exigencies, has been confuted first by Simone de Beauvoir, and then by Carla Lonzi, Luce Irigaray, Judith Butler and Julia Kristeva. The fundamental path followed by these authors was the liberation from the entanglement of traditional culture that swamped women. In spite of some differences, Lonzi's (1974) strategy was the basis of all feminist Italian activities: that is, to speak about experience from the viewpoint closer to life than to theory, because every theory has been made by men and is still driven and overwhelmed by language. The most important thing was not to find "the truth" and the subsequent religious dogma that dedicates any sense of action, but to start rethinking the female way of living and construction of close and social relationships (Ergas, 1986).

Two feminist milestones have been erected from this idea of orienting women's thoughts and agenda towards social and political change: first being actually authentic in life and in relationship with both oneself and others, and secondly assuming agency and creating new political roles. In order to pursue these fundamental aims, parallel to the female rebellion groups, in Italy the "Pratica dell'inconscio" ("practice of the unconscious") took form, a training that corresponds to the phenomenon that was being created in the USA, as an experience of "consciousness raising" or "awareness raising" (Brownmiller, 1999). These further kinds of activities were aimed at beginning a new phase of consciousness-raising and contemplation necessary for women's politicization. There is a substantial difference between female rebellion and unconscious practice groups, however. In the latter, psychoanalysis played a fundamental intellectual role, whilst conversely in the former it was considered a sexist theory. Actually, Carla Lonzi was a strong detractor of the Freudian perspective and across Europe this position gained strength at the time, especially in France, even in the same psychoanalytical circles, thanks to the research of Luce Irigaray (1974), who in *Speculum* defines Hegelian dialectic as patriarchal. According to her point of view, women must recast discourse into a form that does not preserve and imply a masculine subject, harmonizing the machine of language in order to rethink the relationship beyond "phallogocentrism" from which one-only gender categories (*genre*) derive: the masculine one. In this complex operation, finding great alliances in the large international epistemological confutation of psychoanalysis, from Popper (1963) to Deleuze and Guattari (1972), many distortions arose from the sexist concept of the Oedipus complex and penis envy, and a specific space was attributed to the role of motherhood. Nancy Chodorow's work (1974, 1998, 2000) had and still has great importance where the social construction of heterosexuality, femininity, masculinity and motherhood, as they are conventionally understood, are discussed. This perspective shows the potential danger of emphasizing gender differences through mothering, which consists in the justification of the status quo: because women are mothers, women are responsible for the reproduction of gender differences and inequalities. Motherhood is a "natural" (in a Hegelian meaning) predisposition of women, who consequently choose to provide care for others, thus influencing the social structure of relationships and politics (Tong, 1989).

From the French Lacanian school, another important feminist psycho-analytic contribution arose: the perspective of Julia Kristeva (1982), who has presented the concept of "abjection" to define the first original psychological operation necessary to construct individual identity. From her psycho-analytical perspective, abjection is the operation of cutting off the maternal. In Kristeva's viewpoint, to each ego its object, to each superego (which contains interiorized social norms) its "abject", and the "I do separate, reject, ab-ject" is the pre-condition of every possible construction of individual relating society. This concept is more complex and radical than the classical idea of "separation/individuation" discussed by Melanie Klein (1946) and Margaret Mahler (1963), taken from Bion, Bowlby, Winnicott and many other important authors. It is rather linked to the idea of "subjectivity" developed by Judith Butler (1987) that highlights the ambiguity inherent within the term "subject", which as a noun indicates self-determining agency but also as a verb defines the process of being controlled by external will. In Kristeva, the concept of abjection is the precursor of Butler's subjectivity, because it pertains to the dimension of social speaking and its dynamic, as well as being intra-subjective and social. The radical detachment and visceral rejection of the maternal (ob-ject) is what allows the individual to be able to face what is outside of herself/himself. But this first psychological and social operation of separation/individuation requires the painful and tiring processing of original fusional desire for dependence.

From Antigone to womanism: what women must reject?

Simone de Beauvoir in her "Moral Idealism and Political Realism" (2004) defines the consequences of the Hegelian vision of Antigone as the contra-position between ethics and politics, corresponding to the contraposition between family and State. From this interpretative hypothesis, which may be disproved by literary criticism, many feminist reflections have arisen. On one hand, some intellectuals emphasize the political sense of Antigone's act. In particular, the aspect of social rebellion is underlined in Subjects of Desire by Judith Butler, who charts the trajectory from Hegel's Phenomenology to the discussion by some important French philosophers, among which Sartre, Lacan, Deleuze, and Foucault, in order to develop an analysis of the relationship between desire and the unconscious and to define how to manage subjection in the self-development of the individual. In her view, Antigone was executed not because she responded to an affective desire but because of her challenge to the constituted power. On the other hand, some scholars like Kimberly Hutchings (2003), similarly to Luce Irigaray, assume the inter-pretation of Hegelian Antigone as the personification of "divine law" versus

Creon and the "human law." However, there is also a third possibility that combines the two polarities. It is wonderfully described by Trinidad Morgades Besari who rewrote the tragedy in a modern style. Her Antígona (Besari, 1991) was set as the heroine in Africa, in the context of the elected president Macias Nguema, who soon became a tyrant, to show the fundamental duplicity of Sophocles. This narration underlines the indistinguishability between personal and political, of affective and public, of ethical and legal, through the representation of rebelliousness when she violates the prohibition to bury her brother as ordered by Creon, at the risk of her own life. In this way, she symbolizes both female love towards and resistance to male oppression. The three positions converge, however, on the same target: the definition of what is left in the "shadow realm," outside of the public sphere, relegated to the margins and seeking recognition. Antigone is the lack of connection between the order of private relationships and political order and therefore cannot represent anyone, because she herself is not representable in the given cultural system that is incorrect and excessive. The personification of Antigone is possible only in the sphere of womanism since she embodies the "womanist heroine."

The concept of "womanism" can be considered an extension of Irigaray's (1984) political-ethics, where the solution to the mortal execution of Antigone is recognized in the new female way of constructing the real democracy (Irigary, 2000), beginning from an awareness of "being always two" (Irigary, 1992, 1997). In fact, the original concept of "womanism", as indicated by Alice Walker, consists in the existential description of the history of African American women in America and how their "spirit" managed to survive in an oppressive world, despite the abuse and mutilation they endured both in body and in mind. Dimmed and confused by pain, considering themselves unworthy even of hope, the Walkerian subjects in *In Search of Our Mother's Gardens* are women whose legacies surpassed the bondage of slavery, thanks to family and the mother-daughter relationship, considered the basis for shaping individual personalities. Despite this, womanism is an expression of gendered racist and sexist oppression that Black women face, and, as Patricia Hill Collins (1996) notes, it may be a "political distraction", because it exaggerates out-group differences and minimizes in-group variation by assuming a stable and homogenous racial group identity, thus the concept potentially assumes an essentialist position that denies the varied experiences of Black women. We think it indicates a larger risk which has developed inside feminism, not only derived from Black female emancipation. Essentialism is in fact the last legacy of metaphysics upon which the rational theology of historical western religions base their ethical assumptions and their politics, more or less fundamentally.

The question is: if theocratic ethics evoked by essentialism limits the chances of individuation and self-determination of women, why is Antigone still alive?

Conclusion: Abjection of maternal womanism to overcome amoral familism

Womanism indicates not only the primacy of motherhood in Black culture, but also the specificity of women being like Antigone. This is the elective condition of relationships which derive from a culture where intimate relationships converge toward the mandate of motherhood and to amoral familism, to which the act of Antigone can be attributed. The concept of amoral familism by Edward C. Banfield (1958) has been widely refuted but it has also kept alive a strong debate on issues related to social backwardness (Ferragina, 2009). Amoral familism consists in the "maternalization" of the social sphere; it is the reduction of social relationships to the law of blood ties, similar to those of the family and then just dominated by the mother, who is also a woman in turn oppressed and coerced by ideologies that control and limit her agency. The problem is the following: the Hegelian separation of intimate (personal) from social (political) is in function to the separation of roles according to gender differentiation, where the first is given to the realm of women and the second to the male realm. This double discrimination determines the construction of a society where the intimate dimension inflates the social one, and amoral familism, mafia and honor code are the result of this process. In this way, in a society where the differentiation between men and women is strongly related to the Hegelian categorization (that is the traditional one) it confuses the familial with the collective, love with ethics, personal with right, politics with individual interest. What Italian women lack is adequate "abjection of mother," which means the separation/individuation from the affective domination of close relationships, excellently represented by Hegelian Antigone. The Italian experience teaches that the womanist model of Antigone as a political revolution of female love against male power is not effective in changing our sexist society. The catholic promotion of the ideology of male-female complementarity through the limitation of self-determination of real women includes the denial of their right to use science to self-manage their own fertility and sexuality and acts as an illicit occult *deus ex machina* in Italian society. The influence of Catholicism on parliament to deny Artificial Reproductive Techniques (ART) used the consent of Berlusconi, whose government in 2004 banned ART, meanwhile the same prime minister was promoting at a social level, in Parliament, and in the public and private media (almost all seconding his will) the symbol of women as sexual objects, in spite of their education and intelligence, and in private organizing orgies involving immigrant female minors (his so-called "bunga-bunga" parties). It is important to underline what international social research emphasizes with this prohibition, examining religious and legal restrictions on third-party reproductive assistance: Italy became similar to Egypt and multi-sectarian Lebanon with a 2004 law ending third-party reproductive assistance. This result shows the need for understanding the complex interactions between law, religion, local morals, reproductive practices and women's self-determination rights.

The importance of ART is symbolic because, along with contraception, it represents the power that technology gives women to become self-determined individuals, who are not subject to an inflexible law, but only to those laws to which they adhere to by free choice. But if it is so, why is Antigone still alive?

In our opinion the answer to this question is hidden behind the shadow of the mystery of desire that women cultivate as a call to duality, which is intercepted by traditional religious ideologies and translated into political action. Feminism in still too weak and is not able to resist the contamination of traditional ideologies which boast great thinkers.

The experiences of "practice of unconscious" did not last because, although revolutionary and great, de facto they cannot offer major opportunities for reading the deep feelings that move women towards love and motherhood.

In the matricentric and familistic Italian society, it is necessary to renew what is discussed by Nancy Chodorow (1994, 2000) in order to construct subjectivity beginning from the mother-daughter relationship, in order to stop the hegemonic processes of gendering that perpetuates the recreation of traditional roles. It is also necessary to reinvent the "practices of the unconscious," in order to abject to the forms of "being always two" which hampers individuation as self-consciousness and self-determination, pursuing the social abjection of a mothering society. But it is likewise important to understand that women evidently are still not able to resist the idea of carrying a sacred uterus, through which God may still show his power, evidently no longer omnipotent because of technology.

Yes, we know, it is not a simple problem and, importantly, it is not only an Italian one ...

References

Allen, P. (2006). Man-Woman Complementarity: the Catholic Inspiration. *Logos, 9*(3), 87–108.

Alma Laurea. (2007). "Indagine 2008. Profilo dei Laureati 2007." [2008 survey. Profile of Graduates 2007] Retrieved from: http://www.almalaurea.it/universita/profilo/profilo2007/

Banfield, E. C. (1958). *The moral basis of a backward society.* New York: Free Press.

Benedict XVI. (2004). *Lettera ai vescovi della Chiesa cattolica sulla collaborazione dell'uomo e della donna nella Chiesa e nel mondo* [Letter to the Bishops of the Catholic Church on the Collaboration of Men and Women in the Church and in the world]. Roma, Città del Vaticano: Editrice Vaticana.

Brownmiller, S. (1999). *In our time: memoir of a revolution.* New York: Dial Press.

Butler, J. (1987). *Subjects of Desire: Hegelian Reflections in Twentieth-Century France.* New York, Columbia University Press.

Chodorow, N. (2000). Reflections on The Reproduction of Mothering — Twenty Years Later. *Studies in Gender and Sexuality, 1*(4), 337–348.

Chodorow, N. (1994). *Femininities, masculinities, sexualities: Freud and beyond.* Lexington: University of Kentucky.

Chodorow, N. (1978). *The reproduction of mothering.* Berkeley: University of California press.

Conte L., Vinzia, F. & Martini V. (Eds.). (2011). *Carla Lonzi: la duplice radicalità Dalla critica militante al femminismo di rivolta* [Carla Lonzi: a double radical criticism from the militant feminism of revolt]. Pisa: ETS.

de Beauvoir, S. (2004). Moral Idealism and Political Realism. In *Simone de Beauvoir: Philosophical Writings*, edit by Margaret A. Simons, 165–194. Urbana and Chicago: University of Illinois Press.

de Beauvoir, S. (1949). *Le deuxième sexe*, Paris: Gallimard. (eng. trans. *The Second Sex.* New York: Vintage Books, 1989).

Deleuze, F. & Guattari, F. (1972). *Anti-Oedipus.* Paris: Minuit.

Engels, F. (1884). The Origin of the Family, Private Property and the State. Hottingen, Zurich. (MIA Library Source: Karl Marx and Fredrick Engels, Selected Works, Volume Three, retrieved from: http://www.marxists.org/archive/index.htm).

Ergas, Y. (1986). *Nelle maglie della politica: femminismo, istituzioni e politiche sociali nell'Italia degli anni Settanta* [In the fabric of political feminism, institutions and social policies in Italy in the seventies]. Milano: Franco Angeli.

Ferragina, E. (2009). The never-ending debate about the moral basis of a backward society: banfield and 'amoral familism.' *Journal of the Anthropological Society of Oxford, 1(2)*, 141–160.

Hegel, G. W. F. (1977). *Phenomenology of Spirit.* Oxford: Oxford UP.

Hill Collins, P. (1996). What's in a Name? Womanism, Black Feminism, and Beyond. *The Black Scholar, 26*(1), 9–17.

Hutchings, K. & Tuija P. (Eds.). (2010). *Hegel's Philosophy and Feminist Thought: Beyond Antigone?* Basingstoke, UK: Palgrave MacMillan.

Hutchings, K. (2003). *Hegel and feminist philosophy*, Cambridge: Blackwell.

Irigaray, L. (2000). *Democracy begins between two.* New York, London: Continuum.

Irigaray, L. (1984). *Éthique de la différence sexuelle.* Paris: Minuit. (eng. trans. *An ethics of sexual difference.* Ithaca, NY: Cornell University Press, 1993).

Irigaray, L. (1997). *Être Deux.* Paris: Grasset. (eng. trans. *To be two.* New York, London: Routledge, 2001).

Irigaray, L. (1992). *J'aime a toi. Esquisse d'une felicite dans l'Histoire.* Paris: Grasset. (eng. trans. I Love to You: Sketch for a Felicity within History. New York, London: Routledge, 1996).

Irigaray, L. (1974). *Speculum. De l'autre femme.* Paris: Minuit. (eng. trans. *Speculum of the Other Woman.* Ithaca, NY: Cornell University Press, 1985).

ISTAT (2011). *Rapporto annuale: La situazione del Paese nel 2010* [Annual Report: The situation in the country in 2010]. Roma: Istituto nazionale di statistica. Retrieved from: http:// www.istat.it

John Paul II. (1988). *Mulieris Dignitatem: On the Dignity and Vocation of Women.* Roma: Libreria Editrice Vaticana.

John Paul II. (1997). *The Genius of Women.* Washington DC: United States Catholic Conference Publications.

Klein, M. (1946). Notes on some schizoid mechanisms. In J. Mitchell (Eds.), *The selected Melanie Klein*, 176–200. Harmondsworth, England: Penguin.

Kristeva, J. (1982). *Powers of Horror: An Essay on Abjection.* New York: Columbia UP, 1982.

Lonzi, C., Accardi, C. & Banotti, E. (1974). Manifesto di Rivolta Femminile [Manifesto of Female Revolt]. In C. Lonzi (Eds.), *Sputiamo su Hegel: la donna vaginale e la donna clitoridea* [Spit on Hegel: the vaginal woman and clitoral woman]. Milano: Scritti di Rivolta Femminile.

Lonzi, C. (1974). *Sputiamo su Hegel: la donna vaginale e la donna clitoridea* []. Roma: Scritti di Rivolta Femminile.

Mahler, M. (1963). Thoughts about development and individuation. *Psychoanalytic Study of the Child, 18*, 307–324.

Mills, P. J., (Eds.). (1996). *Feminist Interpretations of Hegel.* University Park PA: Pennsylvania State University Press.

Morgades Besari, T. (1991). Antígona. In D. Ndongo-Bidyogo & M. Ngom (Eds.), *La literatura de Guinea Ecuatorial: Antología* (pp. 427–33). Madrid: Casa de Africa.

Popper, K. (1963). *Science: Conjectures and Refutations*. London: Routledge.

Ravera, C. (1978). *Breve storia del movimento femminile in Italia* [A brief history of the women's movement in Italy]. Roma: Editori Riuniti.

Scaraffia, L. & Isastia, A. M. (2002). *Donne ottimiste. Femminismo e associazioni borghesi nell'Otto e Novecento* [Optimistic Women. Feminism and bourgeois associations in the eighth and twentieth centuries]. Bologna: Il Mulino.

Spivak, G. C. (1999). *A critique of post-colonial reason: Toward a history of the vanishing present*. Cambridge, London: Harvard University Press.

Testoni, I. (2012). Essenzialismo tra psicologia sociale e studi di genere: paradossi italiani intorno alla differenza. *Psicologia sociale, 2*, 285–299.

Testoni, I. (2007). *La frattura originaria* [The original fracture]. Napoli: Liguori.

Tong, R. (1983). *Feminist Thought: A comprehensive introduction*. London: Routledge.

Walker, A. (1983). *In Search of Our Mother's Gardens: Womanist Prose*. London: Women's Press Classics.

WAVE. *The Daphne Toolkit*. Retrieved from: http://www.wave-network.org/start.asp?ID=23303

World Economic Forum. *The Global Gender Gap Index 2012*. Retrieved from: http://www3.weforum.org/docs/GGGR12/

Centaurs. A violent masculine myth

Luigi Zoja

In modern law and custom, gang rape has always been considered a crime, whereas in past ages it was a tolerated exception.

The present investigation of the mythical, historical, biological and cultural antecedents of the masculine impulse to rape goes beyond individual pathology. It aims to analyse *collective rape* and the potential model of acritical behaviour that it embodies. This is different from the behaviour of the individual male, who is more or less aware that he is pathological and that he risks a more or less severe punishment.

One would expect gang rape to be an increasingly rare occurrence. But in fact it returned in an uncontrolled form in the Second World War, and since then seems to have become a recurrent epidemic on the margins of former colonies of western nations.

Collective rape is not a mere accumulation of individual rapes: the pathological personality of the individual rapist is aware of the crime it is committing and tries to conceal it, whereas gang rape involves a collective orgiastic syndrome which represses or eliminates guilt feelings. Anyone who decides not to join in is mocked and regarded with suspicion, and may feel as if he is abnormal (Sèmelin, 2005), a small boat in an immense storm.

At a deeper level, gang rape is a surprising re-emergence in the modern age of a classical myth: that of the centaurs. To a centaur there was no difference between sexual life and sexual violence; in his eyes rape was the only true form of sexuality. Nor did he see any distinction between war and orgiastic violence against women; hence today this perverse ecstasy may be termed *centaurism*. The Greek word *centaur* means "one who kills – or spears *(kentein)* – the bull *(tauros)*". There is also perhaps a link with Latin *centuria* (group of a hundred men).

Thus the etymology of the word confirms the menacing elements that underlie the myth: a regression of masculinity to the animal herd and to the physical strength inherent in numbers. In modern historical cataclysms, man may revert to something much more primitive than man, whereas woman remains a woman of, and in, the modern world.

In a wide variety of places and ages, the female identity is characterized by relative stability. The male identity, by contrast, is much more recent; it is linked to society and history, and is therefore more fragile. One of the factors behind the emergence of male dominance may have been the need to deny this precariousness. In the evolutionary scale as far as the level of mammals, females evolve towards an increasingly complex level of care and upbringing of their young; males merely compete for the right to mate. So, on the one hand we see two interlinked roles of mother and educator; on the other, struggle plays the crucial role in defining male relationships and their social position, from one victory to another.

Monogamous and relatively stable families, nuclei in which males also take on responsibilities towards their children, did not emerge until the proto-humans, our direct ancestors. Hence, while in the woman female, maternal identities coexist in an almost harmonious dialectic, in the man the father and the male (the animal) are precariously balanced polarities. The civilized father is the result of a cultural evolution rather than a zoological one: he needs a capacity for abstraction and organization that transcends mere nutrition, as well as protection and improvement. His behaviour is the result of controlling certain instincts; it has a "castratory" function. It expresses its prohibitions in the interests of the family, before degenerating into the abuses of patriarchal power.

For thousands of years Judaeo-Christian values and patriarchal principles provided confirmation and stability for these two never mutually integrated poles of the father and the competitive male. But in the post-modern world, with the breakdown of the family and its traditional values, the thin crust of civilized western patriarchy is eroded; civilized coexistence disintegrates and we see a re-emergence of the pre-paternal male. This is confirmed by the vast predominance of male psychopathies: the lawless male is still here, and can destroy the seemingly impregnable fortresses of history in the space of a moment.

This is the meaning of the stories of centaurs, on the horizons of our history in society and in Greek myth, where the roots of modern thought lie; where the first true western civilization was formed and patriarchal authority reached its most eminent peak. The opposite pole, that of the animal, pre-civilized male, seemed to have been eclipsed, but in fact had only been repressed. In the background of Homer's mythical literature the beast's claws are close and furious; they allude to the instability of the civilized condition, and its links with the realm of instinct.

The centaurs lived in Thessaly, the northernmost extremity of Greece, to which myth attempted to exile a lawless world that was so close in time. They were represented as human beings from head to waist, with the body of a horse without its head and neck grafted on below.

That the story of the centaurs would end badly was clear from the beginning. The centaurs owed their origin to the most violent and impious of men, Ixion. After burning alive his future father-in-law, Deioneus, Ixion is pardoned by

Zeus, who purifies him and grants him immortality and life among the gods. But in the divine palaces Ixion meets Hera and tries to rape her. Hearing of this, Zeus decides to put him to the test, creating a cloud in the image of the goddess. Ixion rapes the cloud and a creature called Centaur is born from his sacrilegious embrace. It was the first creature to have been conceived, as Pindar recalls, without *Charis*: in the dual absence of grace and the passion of love[1].

Erotic raptus and intoxication occasionally appear elsewhere in Greek myth, but only in the centaurs are these two frenzies systematically linked, as a primary form of collective behaviour. The Lapiths, an equally strong and uncontrollable race, ruled by King Pirithous, also lived in Thessaly. When Pirithous married Hippodamia, their neighbours the centaurs were invited to the wedding; one of the centaurs, Eurytion, inebriated by wine and by the bride's beauty jumps on her and abducts her. The other centaurs, also drunk, do the same with the Lapith women, turning the banquet into a battlefield, a bloody clash between two peoples.

In antiquity the myth was a clear warning of the danger of regressing to the animal male. Today, too, mingling alcohol and violence is more often a male than a female characteristic. In antiquity it is rare to find female centaurs[2]; to the Greeks and Romans the centaurs were an insatiable herd, a menacing horde of rampaging drunkards. But the myth also represents them in conflict with two founding fathers, Theseus and the prototypical hero Heracles. Theseus, a symbol of the law-abiding combatant, is not only the architect of the Lapiths' victory over the centaurs; he also participates in the battle against the Amazons, and therefore combats the excesses of the female element too. Although he sometimes indulges in the rape of women (Kerenji, 1958), he is chiefly identified as a just ruler and the mythical founder of Athenian democracy[3]. As a model of patriarchy, Theseus embodies the civilized father, whereas the centaur, the bull and the Minotaur represent the pre-paternal male.

The myth of Heracles, the son of Zeus and Alcmene, takes a similar form. Conceived in one of the many relationships forcibly imposed by Zeus, Heracles is welcomed as a guest by the generous centaur Pholus, who imprudently offers him wine. The smell of the drink attracts other centaurs, who, after drinking the wine, start fighting among themselves and then with Heracles. With his poisoned arrows Heracles unintentionally kills both Chiron, the pedagogue and educator of Achilles and Jason, and Pholus.

Once again, the mythological allusion is to the collective symbol of unjust killings, reflecting the difficulty Greek society had in conducting a dialogue with the instincts (the centaurs): Heracles acts in this case by poisoning and repression, sacrificing Chiron and Pholus, the two most creative elements.

---

1   Pindar. *Pythian Odes* (II). Apollodorus. *Bibliotheca* (Epitome 1, 20).
2   One of the exceptions is Hylonome, who is described in Ovid. *Metamorphoses* (XXII, 405 ff).
3   Thucydides, II, 15.

The warning is clear: the centaurs' meta-human power is that of an anti-deity, an extreme evil capable of annihilating, as we are going to see, even the strongest hero. Just as the god represents the elevation of ecstasy, so the centaur embodies a kind of 'negative ecstasy' comprising aggressive drunkenness and rape. This is not a regression to a literally animal stage: rape, which is often described as 'bestial', is a form of behaviour typical not of animals, but of men (Waal, 2005)[4].

The centaur's alleged bestiality, however, also acts individually, with the same blind frenzy of the herd. This is clear in Heracles' encounter with the centaur Nessus, who is acting as ferryman over the River Evenus: according to one version of the myth, Heracles fords the river first, leaving his young bride Deianeira in the centaur's hands; according to another, Nessus ferries Deianeira across first, leaving Heracles on the bank. In both cases, once the couple is divided, Deianeira feels Nessus's "mad hands"[5] and cries out desperately to her husband on the other bank. Nessus is killed by an arrow from Heracles' bow and as he dies feigns penitence. If Heracles' affections should waver one day, Deianeira need only get him to wear a shirt soaked in the centaur's blood. Deianeira, moved to pity, collects his blood, believing in the miraculous power of love.

Later Heracles goes away and conquers a kingdom, but he also wins the king's daughter: his victory must be ritually honoured with sacrifices to Zeus. Deianeira thinks this is a propitious occasion for using Nessus's blood, and steeps his ritual robe in it. The result is well known: Heracles is burned alive by the shirt steeped in the centaur's blood. On his death he is taken up into Olympus with the other gods; Deianeira, regretting her naiveté, kills herself.

Thus the meta-human centaur is capable only of pathologically violent sexuality; his mind cannot separate itself from instinct, just as in his body the man cannot separate himself from the animal. He is an aggressor who destroys even the bond between a couple, and who sows the seeds of meta-violence in the mind. Once sown there the seeds germinate slowly, as a threat of regression to the psychology of the *male herd* (the *centuria*). That is why the centaur's violence is not identified as a mere animal impulse but is more complex, as in the case of Nessus. It is 'manipulation', which includes the perversion of power, a desire to subdue and humiliate the victim, without any redemption or admission of error. The centaur expresses a dormant and almost ineducable primitive instinct, an impulse of the collective unconscious that may recur in the absence of effective barriers.

---

4   According to de Waal, in some primates (such as the bonobo) rape is unheard of, whereas in
     others (such as the chimpanzee) it is a possible but rare option. The ethologist refers, however,
     to individual acts of violence, never to collective assaults such as those discussed here.
5   *màtaios*: impious, reckless (Sophocles. *Trachiniae*, 565)

Another significant example of this is provided by the myth of the foundation of Rome. At the beginning of his *Life of Romulus*[6], Plutarch gives a propagandistic reconstruction of the capital city's foundation: faced with a continual influx of colonists and a lack of wives, Romulus proclaims that he has discovered the altar of a god named Consus. He invites some neighbouring peoples to the festivities, in particular the Sabines. At a signal from the king, the Romans carry off the Sabine virgins on their shoulders. According to Plutarch this was an act of necessity, not of avidity; in reality, the Romans' act of seizing and raping indigenous women institutionalized the idea of the "melting-pot", the fusion of peoples.

From the point of view of the victims, another equally emblematic archetype for the subject of our investigation occurs in Ovid's *Metamorphoses*. The virgin Caenis, raped by the god Poseidon[7], asks the contrite god to prevent this act ever being repeated by turning her into a man. Poseidon agrees and Caenis becomes the warrior Caeneus, invincible and eager for war.

The just slogan "Never again", used today by the victims of collective rape, has a pathological precedent in the "Caenis syndrome". The victim pays twice over: first she suffers carnal violence, then she vents her fury not on the male who attacked her but on the female beauty and grace that she considers in some sense responsible for the aggression. Here again we have a case of meta-rape, an unconscious but radical introjection of the criminal male. A pathological reaction which sees femininity as the enemy and, to prevent any further aggression, identifies with the aggressor who perpetrated it.

An investigation of the origins of collective rape, which has proved to be in historical terms a *psychological epidemic* and in society a *collective pathology*, is not only concerned with a crime. A *loss of male identity* is the main factor in stimulating gang rape, a phenomenon which jeopardizes the very existence of society. It is a terrible situation which occurs repeatedly, throwing light on mental pathologies in which individuals taken individually contrive to appear sane, but together perform the most unexpected perversions.

The few existing studies on the subject stress, at the root of the phenomenon, a rejection of individual responsibility: alongside the above-mentioned abuse of alcohol and drugs, frequent factors are economic-cultural poverty and the absence of the rule of law and police forces. The main aggravating factor, however, is the state of war rooted in a masculinist, patriarchal culture.

Another important instance of collective male violence were the colonial enterprises. What has been described as the American holocaust (Stannard,

---

6   Romulus is the mythical founder of Rome, just as Theseus is the mythical founder of Athens. For this reason Plutarch in his *Parallel Lives* takes him as Theseus's parallel.

7   It is interesting to note in the context of the present discussion that, like other rapist gods, Poseidon could turn into an animal to disguise himself or deceive female figures, and that his speciality was changing into a horse. Several myths concerning the centaurs are associated with him.

1992; Todorov, 1982; Kiernan, 2007), in the central and southern part of the continent, was carried out by male invaders; they killed the indigenous inhabitants and took their women as concubines. Over the centuries little has been learned about collective rape in war because it has not been discussed as a crime in itself. Ever since the fratricide of Cain or the war between the Greeks and Trojans, violence has destroyed men, but at the same time *generated words*, speeches, tales of bloodshed[8]. Sexual pillaging, on the other hand, *generates silence*; it paralyses the mind by putting the stamp of shame on it and dehumanizing both the victim and the aggressor.

Gang rape is not only a consequence of war getting out of control, but a "programmed" form of behaviour. Today in particular, it tends, partly unconsciously and partly consciously, to accelerate conquest, and sometimes genocide. It can overturn geography and history, like an immense tidal wave that advances invisibly, a fury that spreads hatred and corrupts the uniting impulse which we call eros.

In the twentieth century collective rape of the female population became an integral part of politico-military strategy and no longer simply an immoderate act committed while conquering a particular inhabited area. Although in the past troops had been given the 'right' to pillage as compensation for their efforts, their actions had usually been limited to razing towns to the ground and taking women as slaves.

After the world wars this excess became a permanent means of intimidation aimed at inducing the enemy to surrender and waging psychological warfare which targeted the intimate feelings, the soul of the civilian population, and therefore primarily its women.

The twentieth century saw the emergence of hate campaigns, "genocidal policies" (Brutenau, 2004) ranging from the persecution of minorities to complete massacres. An integral part of these campaigns was the widespread rape of the female population, something the rational plans of governments had difficulty in controlling, because they involved the deepest layers of collective psychology.

The semi-anthropomorphic being of the centaurs, for whom *the only form of relationship with the female is abduction and rape*, embodies a violent seed inherent in the male identity; the spark of an epidemic, which is amplified by the confusion of war and shatters a collective unconscious inflamed by wounds that do not heal when war ends.

Perhaps more than other crimes, rape can attract a voyeuristic attention: and yet the mass media have never really discussed the cultural perversion that underlies the rebirth of "ethnic cleansing" and "ethnic rape" in Central Europe in the 1990s.

---

8   According to the *Odyssey* (VIII, 578-580) the gods caused the Trojan War to take place so that the story of its fall could be told.

And history itself, in conjunction with economic and cultural poverty, fosters the psychological infection: the longer a country has been ravaged by war, the more likely the formation of 'civilian gangs' that unwittingly re-enact the classical myth of the centaur.

At present, the saddest situation exists in Africa. In some states, such as Liberia and Sierra Leone, civil war ended a long time ago, but there are still episodes of gang rape amid a widespread absence of courtship and gentleness on the part of young males. Not only the victims, but the aggressors, not only Caenis, but also the centaur, are radically afraid of love, to the point of institutionalizing a perversion that results in them never finding it.

The modern centaur knows nothing of what happens before and after rape; he is born inside the rape, in the realm of negated affection. Moreover, whereas the individual rapist is almost always a person with profound disorders of the sexual sphere, in centaurian collective rape the rapist is integrated both on the social and on the sexual level. Unfortunately, almost nothing is known about this mentality: there are few studies on the subject, partly because they concern the poorest countries.

Moreover, it seems reductive to talk of "aberrations"; what is really interesting to investigate is the "suffering of the torturer" (Sèmelin, 2005): why does the male seek a sexual relationship with a woman who doesn't want it? What creates a relationship is not so much the orgasm as eros. The male seeks unconsciously not only his own relief, but passion.

In the myth, Apollo continues to pursue Daphne, and Zeus continues to pursue Leda, in a chase that is *an inverted form of passion,* quite distinct from passion. The primitive male wants to overcome the female resistance which gives him a goal of power and makes him exist more than the physical act itself does. The centaur is this too – the suffering torturer in a life lacking in symbols, where myth takes on a pathological and sadistic appearance, partly because of war and the military identity.

It is also striking that many reports describe collective rape in the form of lines of men awaiting their turn (Solzhenitsyn, 2001), as if such rape were a normal activity to perform in wartime. This suggests a collective psychological infection which dulls everything that is personal in the consciousness: awareness and moral judgement.

That is to say, in the herd a conformism is established that alienates the less violent individual, making him imitate the others, or pretend to do so[9]

---

9   During the Vietnam war "Gang rape was seen as essential in the process of bonding the men together *as men*". This conformist reaction, which is unfortunately easy to provoke, needs to be studied in the light of the new discoveries of neurosciences concerning the potential for imitation between primates, but also between humans: the forms into which this violence is channelled are cultural and human, but the mechanism of the group's aggregation and the performance of the group itself seem to be instinctual, atavistic re-editions of group formation in other species too.

(Bourke, 2007). His is a "possessed" ego, in which all willpower is erased and what prevails is the autonomous action of a mythical personage reawoken by the 'intoxication' of the circumstances. In the states of possession and temporary omnipotence the sense of individual responsibility is erased: this *psychological inflation* is matched in the victim by a *psychological deflation*, which may become permanent depression.

Often, when the group identity prevails over the individual, there is a deformation of the perception of others, who are seen not as humans, but as members of another species. The psychoanalyst and anthropologist Erik H. Erikson (Erikson, 1994) described this unconscious experience as *pseudospeciation*.

This is a paranoid attitude which involves the whole group, a deformation that is not perceived as pathological, and which is therefore an inevitable slow prelude to racism in entire populations. For if the evolution of the human species has manifested itself as the result of primarily cultural differentiations, it was in the development of particularities – now only partly erased by globalization – that the cultures themselves have felt and continue to feel a sense of perennial extraneousness with respect to other peoples.

This has been a prelude to continual divarications between "the men" and other groups whose language and customs are not understood and who are labelled as "non-men" or "barbarians". When the differences are too marked and the mind of the person who feels them is unprepared to welcome them, the different groups perceive each other not as cultures, but actually as different pseudo-species.

For this reason, in the face of the deception produced by clothes, language and movements classified as extraneous and bestial, man is alone among animals in killing his own kind: he perceives other men as beings of another species, and therefore no longer men. Instinct almost always prevents animals from killing members of their own species. But the animal species to which man belongs displays such deformed instincts as to believe that killing these "beasts" is permissible and carries no guilt[10] (Zoja, 2009, 2011).

Following Erik Erikson, Eibl-Ebelsfeldt, the founder of human ethology, used the term pseudo-speciation to describe this cultural process[11] (Erikson, 1996) of the *elimination from collective feeling* of the other national and ethnic groups. All inhibitions break down and the 'others' are no longer

---

10 There is a serious error in Hitler's *Mein Kampf* which, as far as I know, has never been discussed: in chapter 11 (a crucial chapter, because it expounds the theory of racism) he argues that different species, such as dogs and cats, do not mate but fight. This is true. But he goes on to apply the argument to difference not of species (*Art*) but of race (*Rasse*), and this is completely false; indeed, as we have seen, Nazism had to invent monstrously strict laws in an attempt to prevent the kind of mating that has always happened, because human beings feel sexual and emotional attraction to one another irrespective of race and nationality

11 The sociologist Kai Erikson, the son of Erik Erikson, preferred the term "psycho-social speciation".

human beings, but things that one is entitled to use, falling into the anti-scientific error that underlies "scientific racism".

For if a species is by definition that group of beings among which mating is fertile, however different in body, language and customs a human being may be, *every human being belongs to the same species*. Mating between dissimilar races may even be more resistant to disease, strengthen the gene pool and prove desirable. Once again literature provides abundant evidence: erotic exoticism has an attraction which has always helped the market of pornography and prostitution.

If sexual and emotional attraction for members of a different group had not existed in every age, Nazism and apartheid would never have had any reason to prohibit mixed marriages. But the mystery of eros, which governs this attraction, intervenes even when the *perversion of a defence instinct* is contaminated with the *perversion of sexuality* in gang rape. Attraction and hatred blend brutally, reawakening the myth of the centaurs.

The psychological epidemic that I have called centaurism leads in wartime contexts to the pseudo-speciation in the male mind, where the woman is seen as a *doubly different pseudo-species*. In the first place she is foreign, in the second place she is doubly other, because she is a woman. In the absence of real relationships because of military misogyny, an encounter with women of the opposing side may cause a strong emotional upheaval because of the memories of calmer situations which they evoke. The act of rape accompanies an attempt at psychological repression which, as with the centaurs, *simultaneously negates the humanity of the enemy and that of the female*.

Like the centaurian mind, the soldier who has been at the front for years is no longer able to relate either to the woman outside himself, or, within himself, to feelings that are gentle and therefore feminine by cultural tradition. However, there survives in gangs of rapists the unconscious "nature" of desiring a victim who respects particular aesthetic parameters: the instinct of destroying the female dual otherness expresses itself in the ambivalence of an erotic impulse which makes the woman a sexual object to be used and exhibited, as in the most ancient forms of pillage.

The exaltation and excitement of the group *superimposes on the instinct of sexuality the ancient instinct of collective hunting* which is presumably deposited deep down in the mind. It is significant that hunting has always been a male activity and that it preceded agriculture: again we see the ancient psychology of the pre-paternal competitive male.

With the later adhesion to military discipline and the obligation placed on the soldier of not fighting against males of the same herd, the need for conquest finds an outlet in a collective hunt for females of the same species; a game which is never random and which often ends with rape: the male animal is exalted and the paternal polarity weakened (Zoja, 2000).

If, then, as many feminist critics have argued, patricentrism in the family, colonialism and war go hand in hand, it is no coincidence that the first half of the twentieth century needed males who specialized in killing. The second half, by contrast, emphasized mechanisms of competition with a view to consumption, foresight and prudence being replaced by the cult of immediate success. Consequently, the new psychological ideal was archaic, the result of a competitiveness which women feel too, both in the professional and in the private sphere.

In Italy the century began with the ideology of Futurism (1909), an international artistic movement which explicitly supported Fascism. In this movement, the rhetoric of contempt for woman and the glorification of danger and violence reintroduced the threat of the centaur to the extent of justifying rape in the conquered country. Woman appeared only as a trophy, and male behaviour which the Greeks had considered out of date thousands of years earlier re-emerged. The novelty was the public affirmation of ideologically justified collective rape, a reminder that the century of technical progress was also the century of moral regression.

Thus the prelude to collective rape was active war propaganda, a circumstance that favoured the birth and proliferation of racial prejudice. A rich array of illustrations also helped to falsify the face of the enemy, who was treated as a potential rapist simply because he belonged to a different race. They were for the most part hybridizations drawing on the unconscious ghosts of the collective western imagination, which were especially common among the more insecure males and those of a lower cultural level.

Up to the Second World War, the stereotype of the black man, structurally and bestially incapable of controlling himself, and therefore a rapist of white women, had pervaded the tales told by Euro-American male chauvinism from the days of slavery to the twentieth century. While it is certainly true that in the history of America both slaves and the descendants of slaves had raped white women, it is equally true that a far more common occurrence, which frequently went unpunished, was the rape by white men of black women who were unable to make any official complaint because of their state of slavery.

In the imagination of western patriarchy, a male of a different race was seen as a threat to its females, whereas the opposite was the case, and this survives as the guilty conscience of civilized society. Even during the six years of the most terrible conflict in human history, the Second World War, the most responsible attitudes were pushed into the background and the predominant one was an aggressive and competitive male psychology.

If, then, mobilization for a 'total war' demanded, from a psychological point of view, regression to pre-civilized states of the unconscious, the consequence was that the exploitation of the female body as a trophy of war fell into a crevice of history. It is no coincidence that the Nuremberg Tribunal examined an unprecedented number of crimes, but not rape, even though this crime was mentioned in the files and had been committed by Nazis too. "After the Second World War, the interest in rapes was hushed up" (Bourke, 2007) and, while the Allies promoted anti-Soviet campaigns, consciences on both sides were guilty and reticent.

After the fall of communism in Eastern Europe, however, a lot of material came out concerning rapes committed in 1945 by the Red Army in Germany, the most serious example of collective rape in human history. With the Soviet advance over the German border, rape became so widespread as to leave no doubt that it had Moscow's approval. It is estimated that at least two million German women were raped, about 200,000 of whom were killed.

There was widespread recourse to abortion: in Berlin this happened in 90% of the cases of unwanted pregnancies. Despite this, it is calculated that from 150,000 to 200,000 children of Soviet fathers were born in Germany the following year. Many were abandoned.

The rapes were remembered only by some extreme right-wing movements and a few feminist groups, but the archives in communist Germany or in Eastern Europe were virtually inaccessible. Had the truth been revealed, acts would have come to light for which the law prescribed decades of imprisonment, and death sentences which would have decimated entire military legions. But many victims did not report the rapes they had suffered because of feelings of trauma and shame, and the political and military authorities remained silent on the subject.

Since centaurism is a collective possession, the ego of individual soldiers is dissolved in the mass; rape becomes an act of war and the defeated a uniform mass. This can be seen again in the actions of the Red Army during its Prussian campaign: the Soviet commanders wanted to annihilate the Germans by routing and exterminating them; it was a campaign of hatred which took the mental deformation of pseudo-speciation to an extreme. If the adversary was female, aggression degenerated into a violent sexual act.

Eros and Thanatos continually stand face to face in the ambivalence of the soldier who wants to cause death and perform the act by which life is sown. As the English historian Beevor has observed, collective rape in the conquest of Berlin went through three stages: the first, a violent encounter during military operations; the second, an orgy of celebrations; and third and last, a tamer phase when the victim is, as before, rewarded with food and small gifts.

Soldiers no longer roamed at large; gradually the ego started to function again, albeit in this less direct form of violence. Of course, the 'other party' also struggled to preserve a trace of lucidity and, as an anonymous diarist wrote[12], searched for "... a wolf to keep the other wolves at bay" (MacDonogh, 2007).

---

12 Anonyma. (1959-2003). *Eine Frau in Berlin. Tagebuch-Aufzeichnungen vom 20. April bis 22. Juni 1945* (from 27 April to the first weeks of May 1945). BTB – München: Random House. Anonyma's text is a quality piece of writing, and is probably the most important

If, then, centaurism can be described as a collective psychological possession, we may note, with regard to Beevor's analysis, that while in the first phase centaurism flares up, in the final phase it gives way to more individual forms of violence: a psychosis which intends to annihilate not so much the enemy's body as the female identity. Evidence of this can be seen in the fall in the birth rate and the silence about the rapes suffered by the women of the DDR occupied by the Red Army: most of them rejected men for the rest of their lives, tragically replicating the sexual rejection of mythical Caenis.

The difficulty rape victims have in re-evoking their trauma inevitably recalls one of the crimes against humanity that are most difficult to put right. But even for rapists memory and repentance may, despite everything, re-emerge decades later, sometimes on an anniversary of the end of the war.

One cannot help wondering whether the centaur, a distant potential model, but one that is likely to reappear in particular historic-cultural circumstances, does not confirm that, as various theories have held, violence lies at the root of human society.

In history, regression to centaurian proto-psychology involves the nullification of individuality in the triumph and exaltation of the military group. Training in military discipline, and in the solidarity which bans fighting between soldiers, may unleash aggressive drives against women. In this sense every war rape is an "ethnic rape" deriving from an instinctive male regression which marks out territory and is intent on spreading its genes as much as possible; thus, violent sexual behaviour coincides with profound problems of male identity.

More than women, men have moulded traditions: and they have considered the female identity as their own property. In war the "centaurization" of soldiers, as a subculture of violence intended to foster the bond between comrades, seems to arise almost autonomously.

Linked to this is the need, less strongly felt by women, to break with nature in order to become citizens of culture: the male intention of building a society is also necessary in order to control his own instinctual condition. The female identity confirms continuity with one's own being; not so the male identity. Like Franz Werfel in his *Fragment Against the Male Sex* (Werfel, 1992), we may affirm that for little girls playing with dolls is an extension of their nature, while the little boy who plays at being a soldier is the product of a culture: and perhaps he could be taught to do something else. In the little girl the game repeats the being; in the male the being repeats the game. This

---

source of concrete information and psychological observations on war rape. In the diarist's entries, rapes decrease in frequency far more quickly than historians tell us today. It is not clear whether this is due to the fact that her experience concerns districts of Berlin with a high population density in addition to troops and military police, or whether the historical research (carried out mainly during the 1990s, half a century later) has concentrated on the most extreme episodes.

confirms a substantial contrast between the female and male modes of being. Natural complementarity is broken. And this generates the crime which has been discussed here, and which has yet to arouse widespread interest and claim a place in the trials of crimes against humanity.

References

Bourke, J. (2007). *Rape. A History from 1860 to the Present*. London: Virago.

Brutenau, B. (2004). *Le Siècle des genocide* [The Century of Genocide] (trans. it. *Il secolo dei genocidi*. Bologna: Il Mulino, 2005). Paris: Colin.

de Waal, F. (2005). *Our inner Ape*. New York, NY: Riverhead Books (trans. it. *La scimmia che siamo*. Milano: Garzanti).

Erikson, E. H. (1994). *Identity. Youth and Crisis (1968)*. New York-London: Norton.

Erikson, K. (1996). On Pseudospeciation and Social Speciation. In C. B. Strozier & M. Flynn (Eds.), *Genocide, War and Human Survival*. Lanham: Rowman and Littlefield (MD).

Kerenyi, K. (1958). *Die Heroen Griechen* [The Greek heroes] (trans. it. *I Dioscuri spartani e i loro cugini. In Gli dei e gli eroi della Grecia*. Milano: Garzanti, 1976). Rhein.

Kiernan, B. (2007). *Blood and Soil: A World History of Genocide and Extermination from Sparta to Darfur* (chapters II and VI). New Haven-London: Yale University Press.

Sémelin, J. (2005). *Purifier et détruire. Usage politique des massacres et genocides* [Purify and destroy. Political use of massacres and genocides]. Paris: Seuil.

Solzhenitsyn, A. I. (2001). *Arcipelago Gulag*. Milano: Mondadori.

Stannard, D.E. (1992). *American Holocaust. The Conquest of the New World*. New York: Oxford U. P. (trans. it. Olocausto americano. La conquista del Nuovo Mondo. Torino: Bollati Boringhieri, 2001).

Todorov, T. (1982). *La Conquête de l'Amérique. La question de l'autre*. (trans. it. La conquista dell'America. Il problema dell'altro. Torino: Einaudi, 1997)

von Münch I. (2009). *"Frau, komm!" Die Massenvergewaltigungen deutscher Frauen und Mädchen 1944/45* ["Woman, come!" The mass rape of German women and girls 1944/45]. Graz: Ares Verlag.

Werfel, F. (1992). *Fragment gegen das Männergeschlecht (1916)* [Fragment against the male sex (1916)]. In Werfel, F. *"Leben heißt sich Mitteilen". Betrachtungen, Reden, Aphorismen (1975)* ["Life itself is blowing". Reflections, speeches, aphorisms (1975)]. Frankfurt: Fischer.

Zoja, L. (2000). *Il gesto di Ettore. Preistoria, storia, attualità e scomparsa del padre* [The gesture of Hector. Prehistory, history, current events and death of his father]. Torino: Bollati Boringhieri.

Zoja, L. (2009). Contro Ismene. Considerazioni sulla violenza [Against Ismene. Considerations on violence]. Torino: Bollati Boringhieri.

Zoja, L. (2011). *Paranoia. La follia che fa la storia* [Paranoia. The madness that makes history]. Torino: Bollati-Boringhieri.

The Goddess Culture: Gylanic [1] Model *versus* Androcratic Model

Claudio Tugnoli

The decline of the Old Europe culture

Archeological findings have supported the hypothesis that a notable cultural turnover in Europe and in the Near East was caused by the invasion of hordes of pastoral nomads known under the name of "Kurgan" (Gimbutas, 2010). These peoples originated in the lands located between the lower Volga and the northern Caucasus [2]. The Kurgan invasions caused deep-set upheavals and

---

1   Neolithic art prior to the Indo-European invasions lacks images depicting war and male domination. Instead, it is all centred on the Goddess and represents a social order in which women play a dominant role as queens, priestesses or clan leaders. In Old Europe, in Anatolia, in Minoan Crete the social order was founded on gylany (from *gy-* woman and *an-* (*andros*) man) - a neologism coined by Riane Eisler, who picks up Marija Gimbutas' interpretation - to indicate a society based on the partnership between the two genders, as opposed to what happens in an androcracy, or in a matriarchy for that matter. The latter two systems feature a dominating hierarchy based on force or on the threat of using it. The gylanic structure, instead, envisages a hierarchy that Eisler defines as an "actualization hierarchy". Actualization hierarchies are "the common system hierarchies, like those of molecules, cells and body organs, for example, that feature a progression towards a higher, more complex and more evolved level of function. Conversely, as can be seen all around us, the main feature of domination hierarchies is the inhibition of the actualization of higher functions not only in the global social system but also in individual human beings" (Eisler, R., *The Chalice and The Blade: Our History, Our Future*, Harper Collins San Francisco, 1987, translated into Italian under the title *Il calice e la spada*, edited by Vincenzo Mingiardi, Frassinelli, Milano 2006, p. 183). This gives rise to Riane Eisler's preference for the gylanic social system that exalts our evolutionary possibilities for the future, unlike androcracy that threatens to lead humanity towards planetary disaster.

2   The term "Kurgan" means "barrow", i.e. a rounded mound, namely the typical burial sites of the Kurgan culture. Archeological research has found many examples of these that date back to the Copper Age and to the Bronze and Iron Ages. This indicates that the populations of Indo-European language did not originate in Central or Northern Europe or in the Balkans. The Kurgan people moved in the period ranging from the 5th to the 3rd millennia

radical changes in what was Europe at that time: its civilization was suddenly interrupted and destroyed between the 5th and the 4th millennia B.C. (Gimbutas 2010, 72). The inhabitants of Old Europe were sedentary horticulturists who lived in unfortified and unarmed dwelling clusters. Their civilization was egalitarian, matrilineal and matrilocal and overall essentialy peaceful. Conversely, the Kurgan were herdsmen whose society was based on a patrilinear organization. They lived in small seasonal settlements and reared their animals on a free range basis. The divide between the old Europeans and the Kurgan was evident not only in family life and in material conditions, but also in their beliefs. While the Europeans envisaged a Creative Mother as the personification of the feminine principle that represented the agricultural cycle of birth, death and regeneration, the Kurgan on the contrary upheld heroes and warrior gods, divinities that supported lighting and thunder. While the old Europeans lacked weapons, the Kurgan, like all known Indo-Europeans, exalted the lethal power of weapons and especially of sharp blades of all shapes and sizes, ranging from the knife to the sword, from the axe to the stiletto. The Kurgan civilization was able to purify itself of the violence generated from its midst only by means of sacrificial rituals – the physiological unit of measurement of expulsion of violence and of its sacralisation into typically male divinities. Marija Gimbutas states that the typical Kurgan tombs, covered by a mound of stones, conceal various skulls of children as well as deep holes containing piles of skeletons that are evident indications of mass sacrifices, i.e. common forms of human sacrifices, no signs of which have ever appeared in Old Europe (Gimbutas 2010, 90).

This leads to two radically opposite ideologies, the Old European and the Indo-European, which have been defined as a result of thirty years of archeological research (Gimbutas 2005, 2008, 2010). The clash between Old Europe and the Proto-Indo-European Kurgan culture is the prelude to the passage from the matrilinear order to the patrilinear one, from a theocracy to a military patriarchy, from equality to inequality, from the religion of the chtonic Goddess to the Indo-European pantheon dominated by male divinities that lived in the sky. This finally led to the creation of a new civilization that settled in central Europe, consisting of indigenous and Kurgan elements. The two substrates, consisting of the Old European and the Indo-European elements, still coexist in the myths, in the symbols and in the language despite the intrinsic opposition between the two belief systems.

The Proto-Indo-European pantheon differed deeply from the Old Europe one in that it mirrored the hierarchical and layered organization of a society divided into dominants and dominated, at the summit of which one found the three dominating classes: the sovereigns, the priests and the warriors. The

---

from Eastern Europe and from the Northern Caucasus, lands that have revealed a large quantity of archeological findings, especially thanks to the work of Marija Gimbutas.

male divinities were mostly represented mounted on a horse and armed. They embodied the creative function of life, while the female divinities played only the roles of wives of the gods. Religion was based on the Sun and on celestial phenomena such as thunder and lightning. They were celestial divinities, and as such in Bronze Age depictions carried splendid weapons (knives, swords, shields), adorned themselves with copper or gold breast plates, copper-plated belts, gold or amber discs. The god of death was terrifying. Indo-Europeans glorified sharp blades and the speed of the arrow and the lance. With the touch of his lance, the god of death and of the underworld donated a glorious death to the hero.

The Kurgan upheld the idea of the individual, of the male and of the warrior, who deserved a burial with full honours. In Old Europe, instead, the two genders were buried together. This points to widespread sexual egalitarianism and the scarce importance of the individual in the cycle of birth, death and regeneration. The passage of the Kurgan into the afterworld was one way only towards a world of the dead in which the soul would remain forever without any chance of rebirth. Food and objects were placed in the tomb based on the belief that the individual continued its life in the afterworld, albeit in the shape of a larva but preserving the same status held while on Earth. The Kurgan's underworld was totally separated from life on Earth and no one came back from it. Such irreversibility contrasted with Old Europe beliefs in which "death was inextricably intertwined with the cycle of life, death and regeneration in which all individuals were equal" (Gimbutas, 2010, 149).

The sacralization of violence in the Kurgan system

The link between the belief in life after death and regular sacrificial ceremonies reveals itself to be interesting and fertile when compared to the probable absence of sacrifice in pre-Indo-European culture, in which the matrilinear structure prevails. Indeed, the sacrificial system (Girard, 1980) could be the feature of a male domination society that is strongly hierarchized and which keeps women in a position of subordination. This latter element is ideologically justified by the conclusive myth in *Timaeus*, by which living creatures, woman included, are all indicated as coming from the degeneration of primigenial men (Plato 2000, 270-275; Tugnoli 2012). The Kurgan's patriarchal society could have triggered the scapegoat system, by means of which a victim deemed guilty of widespread violence is expelled and sacralized. The myth is the tale in which the solution to the problem of violence is devised, practiced and justified by the dominant male element. The asymmetrical character of the relationship between man and woman that defines sexual difference in the Kurgan society perfectly matches the active/passive, persecutor/victim dichotomy typical of the archaic scapegoat system, precisely how it has been reconstructed by scapegoat anthropology.

One can find consonance between the social order of Old Europe and evangelical precepts, based on the refusal of violence, on the opposition to evil in all its forms, on the rejection of retributive violence. The "female" character of Christ, his "idiocy" and hypersensitivity to violence, the Mother of Christ herself, survival and rebirth of the living Goddess, can be interpreted as the unequivocal signs of the recovery of the civilization of Old Europe. The scapegoat mechanism is unhinged by the Christ, the "son" of the Goddess. Following this line of interpretation, stemming from Girard's anthropological essays, the founding lynching is attributed essentially to the Kurgan system. Its archaic character is therefore relative, not absolute, since archaic cultures like the Old European one have existed and have set up social orders based on non-violence. In short, we can surmise, therefore, an ideal, if not real, continuity between the ideology of Old Europe, the unveiling of the victim's innocence in the Hebrew Bible and the revelation of Christ. Scapegoating, the founding lynching, the divinization of the killed victim, the archaic myth, the sacrificial system (Girard 1980, 1998) all seem to be aspects of the Kurgan culture, accustomed to expelling violence with violence. Mimetic reciprocity can lead to violence only when the opponents are open to rivalry, and this is possible only if they conceive their own identity as entirely separated and independent from any other otherness, namely affected by fixism and identity-centered substantialism that turns the Ego into an impregnable fortress. Within this context, the subjects are alternative and disjunctive, not interdependent and intersecting; property is exclusive, not inclusive; power is dominating, not cooperative; even the opposition between male and female is signed by inequality.

The overturning of the mythical scheme starts with the Hebrew Bible and peaks in the Gospels (Girard 1987, 2003). Whereas in myth the victims are represented as truly responsible of the crisis and as the guilty parties, and even the victims themselves believe they have committed the crimes they are accused of while the persecutors are just and justified, in the Hebrew and Christian Scriptures the crowd is accused of having persecuted and lynched innocent victims. In the Bible's prophetic passages, the crowd's perspective is contested. Job himself is unjustly pushed towards tragedy and the entire community rises against him. Joseph's brothers behave with him as a crowd blinded with hate. Many prophets are persecuted and lynched by the crowd. While the myth denounces the killed victim's crimes, the Hebrew Scriptures denounce the crowd's crimes. The Gospels use a narrative sequence that is identical to that of myths. They begin with the crisis of the Hebrew State subjected to Roman domination. This crisis will culminate in the drama of a single victim, Jesus, killed and then deified by his followers. The difference, however, lies in the fact that the Gospels champion a point of view that is the opposite of that of myths, and namely that the victim is innocent and the persecutors are guilty of the highest injustice (Girard 1983, 1998, 2011). In their opposition to the archaic myth form, the Gospels represent the rebirth of the Goddess culture.

Plato's myth of the Metals

Old Europe's culture was submerged by the Kurgan invasion that consisted in repeated incursions starting in the 5th millennium B.C.. It resulted in the transformation of the gylanic culture into an androcratic one. The egalitarian, pacifist, matrifocal cultural model founded on compassion and on the veneration of the ability to *give life* (Eisler, 2006) was slowly, albeit not evenly, replaced by the Kurgan model in which the relationships between sexes were hierarchized. The hierarchy, based on domination/submission, extended to the whole of society and influenced the relationships between different classes and races. The Kurgan's androcratic model sacralizes violence, i.e. the ability to *take life*, as a tool for maintaining order via domination. Associated to male values, the androcractic model holds its control over society through violence. The original lynching and the periodical sacrifice of scapegoat victims are thoroughly coherent with the Kurgan androcratic culture but not with the opposite model represented by the gylanic culture. Only societies that keep the order using domination – male over female, rich over poor, governors over governed, strong over weak, whites over blacks – can generate within the scapegoat mechanism. Scapegoat anthropology adequately explains the functioning of an androcratic society in which the persecutors/victim dichotomy is a constantly present device, is the central and essentially dualistic core of the hierarchical order, ready to enter into action whenever the indifferentiation process (the *all against all*, according to the renowned Girardian formula) threatens to dismantle the entire social structure (Girard, 1980, 1987). The highly hierarchized androcratic order is forced to create a mythological justification for the legitimization of the division/opposition between society's different elements. In *Politéia*, Plato has Socrates explain that the only function of the origin of the three classes from three metals (gold, silver, iron/bronze) is to put an end to any objections and to make everyone accept their belonging to a given class without further discussion so that they will diligently perform the tasks typical of their rank and without challenging the order of the State (Plato, 1999, 217-219). The Phoenician tale, in which they are to be persuaded of the necessity to obey the established order, narrates that native earth gave birth to men already prepared by nature to carry out exclusive tasks. By this means, guardians and defenders, gold and silver men, are predestined prior to birth to rule over and protect the land they live in as if it were their mother. In this myth, the "gylanic" element is represented by the idea that men are born from mother earth (reminiscent of the Goddess) and by the fact that they are all *brothers*. This entails that the gold and silver men owe their brothers their protection and help. Guardians and defenders shall be instructed coherently with their actual birth. Indeed, Plato's *Politéia* states that guardians and defenders shall own nothing (money, lands, goods of any kind) and shall share the women. This means that their offspring will not have a known father and barely a mother, as if they derived directly from the universal uterus of Mother Earth. The heritage of Old Europe is embodied in the gylanic culture as the expression of non-violence and of roots in the earth. Traces of this are latent also in Plato's constitution whereby guardians and defenders must not possess anything but must share everything, because if they were to purchase houses, lands and other property they would be administrators of their wealth, hateful owners, not allies of their fellow citizens, ready to attack them and fight them as enemies instead of taking care of them. Despite the dominion operated by the opposite Indo-European culture that is aggressive and founded on the pre-eminence of the individual, the religion of the Goddess and its symbols survive like an underground stream and continue to influence not only philosophy but art and literature as well.

The androcratic sacrifice and the gylanic sacrifice

Riane Eisler's cultural transformation theory proposed the evolution of civilization towards an original gylanic model as the obligated direction for the over-coming of the disaggregation caused by the adoption of the androcratic model (Eisler, 1996, 6). Eisler observes that societies that differ greatly in terms of other aspects (such as Hitler's Germany, Khomeini's Iran, Japan's Samurai and the pre-Columbian Aztecs) all share a common trait, they are societies with "a generally hierarchical and authoritarian social structure featuring high degrees of social violence and especially warmongery" (Eisler, 1996, 9). The expulsion of a victim is an integral part of the androcratic system, the physiology of which constantly needs to "defecate" the violence that accumulates in the social organism.

Eisler mentions that Abel's sacrifice (the slaughtered sheep), which represents the shepherd and stockbreeding populations, pleases Yahweh more than the offering of fruits of the ground customarily offered by Cain. By overturning historical reality, in which the pastoral populations imposed their own model of domination and of sanguinary sacrifice, the Bible attributes the killing of the brother to Cain. According to Eisler, therefore, there has been a very clear distortion of the tangible facts (i.e. the crushing of the agricultural peoples by the pastoral and stockbreeding invaders) with the intent of concealing actual responsibilities.

In androcratic societies, sacrifice reveals the concept of power intended not as the power of giving life but of taking it, not as the capacity to alleviate suffering but of providing it, and not as the opportunity to help the weak but of repressing them further. In this society, founded on violence and on force, fathers have the power to sacrifice their children (the fact that the sacrificing subject is always a male is significant). Eros, just like women, is placed under male control, although the desire for a harmonious union between man and woman never completely regresses. This longing is evident in Orpheus' myth: it's not the warrior ready to kill and to seduce and abandon women, but rather the poet and the musician. Orpheus expresses men's aspiration to "escape from a culture that imprisons them in a stereotype of masculinity absorbed in predominance and violence" (Eisler, 1996, 169).

The aim of this article is not to explore the controversy regarding the practice of sacrifice. We can safely say, however, that there has never been a society that fully exemplifies the partnership model, not even the Cretan one. Although the partnership model is not compatible with the practice of sanguinary sacrifice, it's possible the societies that have adopted the cooperative model have practiced sacrifice in exceptional circumstances. The same can be said for the opposite model, whereby the societies that have followed the androcratic model that features the violent method of expulsion of violence, have been known to renounce sanguinary sacrifice due to contamination with the values of non-violence. We still see the clash between the two in present times: on the one hand we have the environmentalist and pacifist philosophy, and on the other the war and destruction ideology that transforms technology into an increasingly sophisticated means of domination and extermination. In societies based on the partnership model, sacrifice is not abolished for the simple reason that this model envisages that kind of dedication to one's fellowmen and that kind of *renunciation* of power and of individual achievement that can be aptly defined as *self-sacrifice*. It could be said that partnership societies renounce sacrifice because they are founded on the willingness of all its components to self-sacrifice. Self-sacrifice so that another can live is antithetical to the sacrifice of another life – the victim deemed the guilty party – so that the victim's killers can go on living. In an androcratic society, there are various forms of real or figurative scapegoating, all of which are based on the concept of expelling violence with more violence. Self-sacrifice and the sacrifice of a victim are diametrically opposite processes. While self-sacrifice is altruistic, the sacrifice of a victim is egotistic. Indeed, the former expresses love for the fellow man and renouncement of one's own benefit of any kind, physical survival included. The latter is the repetition of the original lynching, the conclusion of a process of persecution and of expulsion carried out to the detriment of an innocent victim on which is concentrated all of the hate accumulated within the society. The person performing self-sacrifice is fully aware of what he or she is doing and of its consequences. Conversely, the scapegoating mechanism is dominated by the unconscious; the persecutors are self-deceived with regard to the victim's guilt, believing it to be incontrovertible. They are unaware of the injustice they are perpetrating, of the *nefandum* performed at their hands. As soon as they become aware of it, they cease all acts of persecution. Indeed, "a scapegoat is had only by those who do not know they have it" (Girard, 1987).

In the episode of King Solomon's judgement in *1 King*, not only does the mother give up her son but also accepts the consequences of the accusation of having lied. This episode represents the interruption of a scapegoating event prospected as being the only viable solution to the opposite and symmetrical claims of the two women regarding the live child (Girard 1987; Tugnoli 2001). The cutting of the child in two and the distribution of the two halves to the two women would turn the live child into the innocent victim on which is focused the violence of King Solomon's court and of the two women. Self-sacrifice consists of the renunciation, or a set of renunciations, which the individuals must be capable of accepting, with the aim to adapt themselves to those with whom they must cooperate in order to establish a relationship of reciprocity and mutuality. In partnership societies, conflicts are re-absorbed *a priori* through self-sacrifice. At a certain point, the wisest one steps back, gives up trying to impose his or her reasons and rights, as long as someone else can benefit from the renunciation. In the name and for the love of the collectivity, it is possible to renounce ownership, forgo being right and ultimately give up life. In Eisler's terms, the binary opposition of self-sacrifice/egotism is opposite to the dualisms mutual/dominating and gylanic/androcratic.

The Gospels' restoration of the Culture of the Goddess

If we consider Biblical tradition, we see that *Genesis* contains two versions, or traditions, regarding the creation of man and woman. In the first, *Gen* 1:27, the "Eloist" version, God creates man in his own image, making man and woman simultaneously. In the second, *Gen* 2:21-22, the "Yahwist" version, God first creates man, then sees that Adam needs a companion and so "extracts" Eve from Adam's rib. The Eloist tradition represents the egalitarian concept, while the Yahwist tradition shows a hierarchical vision of the relationship between male and female. The two tales about the creation of mankind are so deeply diverse that we can speak of a veritable discrepancy. Eisler expresses no doubts when she says that this discrepancy, like others in the Bible, can be attributed to the conflict obviously still present between the memory of the egalitarian concept present in the ancient culture and the new androcratic vision that the ruling priesthood set up to make sure that the people accepted the hierarchical and authoritarian organization of the new culture (Eisler, 1996).

Eve's guilt consisted in her unwillingness to renounce the old cult. This means woman required greater punishment than Adam, as if she were doubly guilty because she is a woman linked to the Goddess cult that the new order wished to wipe out and submit. She was therefore condemned to unthinkable suffering for the rest of eternity, "and in eternity condemned to be dominated by this vindictive God and by his earthly representative, man" (Eisler, 1996, 154). The new, emerging culture, inspired by values that are opposite to those of the previous culture founded on the cult of the Goddess, necessarily required discrediting of the Goddess by depicting as abominable the figures associated with her – especially the snake and archetypal woman. The new dominators had to immediately brand any form of success/claim by women of the autonomy and dignity, that the reproductive function recommended should be vested in her, as essentially evil and ruinous for the whole of humanity. In this way, woman lost the right to choose her partner and acquired the duty to obey male rule. Eisler suggests that the story of the expulsion from the Garden of Eden immediately acquires a precise meaning when it is interpreted as "an androcratic tale on how the egalitarian population that adored the Goddess, dedicated to agriculture (or horticulture), were conquered by bellicose sheepherders and dominated by males, and on how this marked the end of woman's sexual and reproductive freedom" (Eisler 1996, 156, note 39).

The figure of Jesus, together with his teachings, his assiduous and respectful interaction with female figures and his rejection of consolidated hierarchies and of formalities, was totally in contrast with the androcratic ideology. The novelty and extraordinary nature of the revelation contained in the Gospels are not dimmed by the fact that the contents of Jesus' teachings have been anticipated by the gylanic concept of human relationships. Believers and non-believers alike can consider as significant the return of values derided and rejected by the androcratic system and yet never completely eradicated. The Gospels are witness for both – believers and non-believers – of their absolute superiority in relationship to the cult of power and of organised abuse of power. The class of priests that condemns Jesus to death cannot accept that someone claims to have acquired the knowledge of the word of God directly, without the mediation of their hierarchy. No compromise is possible, only a direct clash between Jesus, the incarnation of the gylanic values, and the class of priests that represents an androcratic tradition, founded on the preservation of hierarchical order by means of force. The reaction of the dominating culture to the rebirth of the ancient concept of the Goddess could not be less violent. The banishment of the gnostic Gospels is the expression of the irritation with the idea that individual knowledge is a sufficient means of access to the divine, outside the boundaries of hierarchy. As paradoxical as it may seem, Jesus is therefore the first heretic in the history of Christianity. In fact, since he is the expression of the cult of the Goddess and is open to knowledge in all directions, Jesus is destined to suffer the retaliation of the established authority that does not tolerate critical individualism and autonomous knowledge. The class of priests, like Yahweh in the *Genesis*, forbids personal and direct study of the Scriptures because it fears critical knowledge, and punishes with extreme cruelty anyone who dares practice scientific research. The sin that Yahweh punishes with the expulsion from Paradise is the same as that committed by Jesus who is then punished with the death sentence. So if we say that Jesus has come to redeem Adam and the entire community from sin, we can certainly understand the sense of the *salvation* that Jesus promises above all by means of *knowledge*. Jesus redeems from the original sin (i.e. having eaten from the tree of knowledge of good and evil) with his teachings, which are the revelation of the "things hidden since the foundation of the world". This knowledge, Jesus' knowledge, is announced to the world with the words and with life itself. Indeed, he does not back out, but he allows himself to be put to death for the love of truth, for the innocence of the victim and for the falsity of the mythic culture (i.e. androcratic) founded on violence. Jesus is banished for his love of knowledge and for having violated the rule that bans access to the knowledge of good and evil.

Conclusion: towards the assertion of gylanic values

History demonstrates that the exaltation of war and of aggressiveness has always been accompanied by contempt for woman and for female values. The glorification of war and the use of force points to an androcratic concept of virility: the hero is not the caregiver, but rather the figure that unhesitatingly exerts brutal violence. Certainly, in the course of a conflict there can be episodes that resort to female values, such as self-sacrifice, but they remain sporadic moments in a chain of events that qualify as a series of retaliations. The fact that women have been systematically excluded from the exercise of power because they inspire values that are incompatible with the androcratic organization of society is not denied, – writes Eisler – by the fact that some of them have reached dominating positions (like Indira Gandhi, Margaret Thatcher, etc.), because they have been able to exert power at that level mostly due to having shown that they possess male virtues such as aggressiveness, cynical insensibility, professional cool, etc.. The 20th century has witnessed, in the Sixties and Seventies in the Western world, the spread among young people of attitudes contrary to war, heroism and virility of authoritarian hierarchical type, but the system reacted with antibodies aimed at quashing the new attempt at rebirth of the Goddess cult. All of the forces of reaction, the militarist and interventionist right wing, the high finance, the arms industry, etc. marched united in the same direction, resulting in the rebirth of the traditional culture based on the submission of women, as demonstrated by the upsurge in violence against women of the last few decades (Eisler 1996, 249-250). In fact, the amount of violence committed against women is directly proportional to the threat of the feminist movement to the androcratic system, now that all over the world women's freedom from male over-bearingness walks in step with the demand for equal rights for all subjects and for the mandatory safeguarding of the dignity of every human being. The gylanic/androcratic conflict that re-ignited in the Middle Ages, in the Italian Renaissance and in the 20th century, is still under way.

In prehistoric religion, everything is sacred and spiritual, including the human body and sex. Our prehistoric ancestors celebrated with sexual rites the return of life each year in Spring. From a principle that moves the entire universe, sexuality has been degraded to the status of necessary evil, source of sin, despicable lust. Violence against women has reached colossal proportions throughout the world, and the awareness we have of it, together with the analysis of the causal factors implicated in its historical/cultural origin, make it an urgent issue and justify any effort made to solve it from within, namely by means of a deep-rooted change at cultural, ethical and anthropological level. What is required is a radical change capable of removing the normalization of violence, the familiarity with horror, the widespread association of sexuality and of sexual excitement with rape, violence and the use of women as a tool for male pleasure. Individuals that are excited by violence and by cruelty are the extreme, fine-filtered product of the androcratic culture that dominates the planet. Sex as a tool for establishing male power sees its most eloquent expression in Don Giovanni and in Casanova, who when relating the maneuvers he uses to conquer his prey, confesses that it is not the sex that excites him but rather "the overcoming of the women's resistance and the imposition of his will" (Eisler 1996, 308).

An androcratic society is based on an official psychology of the same kind. Otherwise, what other explanation could there be for the recommendation in psychology that man avoid identifying with the mother and actually separate himself from all forms of femininity? Eisler quotes the psychologist Knoll Evans to remind us that "the forbiddance to identify with and therefore have empathic relations with the mother is a way of teaching a man not to feel 'gentle' or 'female' emotions, and therefore not to have empathy-based relations with any woman – not even, as cited by Roszak, with 'the woman most desperately in need of liberation, the 'woman' that every man has locked away inside the dungeons of his psyche'" (Eisler, 1996, 313).

References

Eisler, R. (1987). *The Chalice and The Blade: Our History, Our Future*, Harper Collins San Francisco, translated into Italian under the title *Il calice e la spada*, edited by Vincenzo Mingiardi, Frassinelli, Milano 2006.

Eisler, R. (1995). *Sacred Pleasure*, translated into Italian under the title *Il piacere è sacro*, edited by Maura Pizzorno, Frassinelli 1996.

Gimbutas, M. (2005). *The Living Goddesses: Religion in Pre-Patriarchal Europe*, edited by Miriam Robbins Dexter, translated into Italian under the title *Le dee viventi*, edited by Martino Doni, Medusa, Milano.

Gimbutas, M. (1989). *The language of the Goddess*, translated into Italian under the title *Il linguaggio della dea*, by Selene Ballerini, new unabridged and updated edition, Roma, Venexia 2008.

Gimbutas, M., (2010). *Kurgan. Le origini della cultura europea*, prefaced by Carlo Sini, translation and editing by Martino Doni, Medusa, Milano.

Girard, R. (1972). *La violence et le sacré*, translated into Italian under the title *La violenza e il sacro*, by O. Fatica and E. Czerkl, Adelphi, Milano 1980.

Girard, R. (1978). *Des choses cachées depuis la fondation du monde*, translated into Italian under the title *Delle cose nascoste sin dalla fondazione del mondo*, by R. Damiani, Adelphi, Milano 1983.

Girard, R. (1987). *Le bouc émissaire*, translated into Italian under the title *Il capro espiatorio*, by Ch. Leverd and F. Bovoli, Adelphi, Milano.

Girard, R. (1998). *La vittima e la folla. Violenza del mito e cristianesimo*, passages selected and translated by Giuseppe Fornari, Santi Quaranta, Treviso.

Girard, R. (2002). *One Long Argument from Beginning to the End*, translated into Italian R. Girard, *Origine della cultura e fine della storia. Dialoghi con Pierpaolo Antonello e João de Castro Rocha*, edited by E. Crestani, published by Raffaello Cortina, Milano 2003.

Girard, R. (2010). *Gewalt und Religion. Ursache oder Wirkung. Herausgegeben, mit zwei Gesprächen und einem Nachwort von Wolfgang Palaver.* translated into Italian, *Violenza e religione. Causa o effetto?*, by A. Castelli, edited by Wolfgang Palaver, published by Raffaello Cortina, Milano 2011.

Plato (1997). *La Repubblica*, translated by Franco Sartori, Introduction by Mario Vegetti, notes by Bruno Centrone, Laterza, new abridged edition 1999, 414 and ff., pages 217 and ff.

Plato (2000). *Timeo*. Introduction, translation and notes, supplementary data and appendix of iconography by Giovanni Reale, appendix of references by Vincenzo Cicero, Bompiani.

Tugnoli, C. (2001). *Girard. Dal mito ai vangeli.* Edizioni Il Messaggero, Padova.

Tugnoli, C. (2012). *Le radici culturali della violenza sessuale.* Ines Testoni, Michael Wieser, Adriano Zamperini, Paolo Cottone (a cura di), *Vittima e carnefice nella violenza di genere: dalla violenza sessuale intrafamiliare alla violenza di comunità / Persecutor-victim relationships in gender violence: from intrafamiliar rape to community violence,* 2012.

Awareness of victimization and request for help: Two moments of the same path

Marco Monzani

The victim according to Emilio Viano

Emilio Viano, teacher of criminology and victimology at the University of Washington and director of the International magazine *Victimology* defines the victim of an abuse as

> "Any subject injured or that has suffered wrongdoing on the part of others, **who perceives herself to be a victim,** who shares the experience with others looking for help, assistance and compensation, who is recognized as a victim and who presumably is being helped by public, private or collective agencies/structures" (Viano, 1983;1989).

The elements that make up the definition "victim" are, therefore, according to the author:

1. the damage sustained;

2. awareness of victimization;

3. the request for help;

4. the ratification;

5. the assistance (aid).

The damage sustained. Damage refers not only to financial damage, viewed only in monetary terms, but any form of damage, from financial, to physical, biological, psychological, and moral, as well as the much discussed and now reformulated existential damage. Fortunately, in recent years, it has become more apparent that "wounds that don't bleed (emotional wounds) are often more painful than wounds that bleed (physical wounds)…" (Amodio et al., 1975).

    Awareness of victimization. Many subjects suffer unfair treatment but, for various reasons (cultural, religious, social etc.), they don't perceive themselves as victims; not only do some of these not view themselves as victims but, sometimes, they tend to blame themselves for the situation in which they have to live and put up with (Vezzadini, 2006).

An obstacle to awareness is without doubt represented by a cultural system of silence, that legitimises and justifies the victimization, that presents such behaviour as tolerable or as "not so bad after all..."; this complicates a situation which is already in itself complex and painful (Adami, Basaglia & Tola, 2002).

The difficulty of recognizing victimhood may arise from an unconscious ideology. Some victims cannot imagine alternatives to their situation so do not have the opportunity to rebel (Testoni, 2007).

The request for help. Sometimes the victims, fearing retribution or reprisals that may be worse than the actual abuse, even though they know their rights, tend not to report the abuse and, more generally, tend not to ask for help. They may have sunk into a strange reality that legitimises their status, become "accustomed" to living in a situation of unjust suffering and submission, and rather than risk making the situation worse, they prefer to continue living a life of pain, at least "secure" in knowing what will happen tomorrow.

Victimization is a "dynamic" experience that evolves in a particular way; it's not an instantaneous experience, even when it is, unfortunately, no longer a vague possibility but a living reality.

To begin the 'liberation' from a given type of victimization (whatever it may be) it is necessary, though, to create adequate situations (financial and social) in order to be able to implement and sustain a certain type of project.

The ratification. The ratification, suffice to say, the "formalization" of the status of the victim on the part of the relevant institutions, is a necessary prerequisite before the victim may benefit from the help and the facilities provided for by law and which are reserved for those meet the criteria for this category (Monzani, 2011).

Assistance (aid). If the victim does not report the situation in which she is living, and / or if the persons around her do not recognize her status as victim, the victimization and the blame could be increased and thus multiply the effects.

Often the first help rendered on the part of significant figures re-establishes in the victims a sense of trust in society and neighbour, and this helps them to take that indispensable step to overcome the situation, that is reporting it to the authorities (Saponaro, 2004). Failing to overcome the acute phase of the victimization means that one risks having to live all her life, or a good part thereof, with difficulties that may powerfully limit her self-realization. Or more simply, that might impede her from living a 'normal' life; in a word, to quote the 'World Health Organization', that could provoke a significant worsening in the quality of life.

The victim in denial. Some victims deny their situation of victimization. Denying does not mean not knowing, or not having the cognitive tools and/or the culture to understand the situation which they are in; **denial means not wanting to accept what she knows,** and it also means, "blocking out awareness." (Monzani, 2011).

When one denies her actual situation of victimization, as has already been said, one also denies the chance of asking for, and obtaining, the necessary help to get out of the situation.

The victim in denial (Monzani, 2010) has all her cognitive tools, aside from those of cultural and social character, to enable her to understand her situation, but " she prefers" (subconsciously) to deny everything to herself, as well as to others (De Cataldo, Neuburger & Gulotta, 1996). If she is witness to the same behaviour committed against other people, she recognizes it as victimization, but she denies it when facing the same treatment herself. And the reasons for such denial should be looked for, fundamentally, within the pain that she suffers as she "emerges into awareness" of what is happening to her; pain tied, for example, to watching specific sentimental links considered indispensable, crumble; to the necessity of accepting that the person she trusted until a few moments before, is revealed as her predator; to the pain of having to agree to start life anew, with all the consequential problems (psychological, economical, social, care of children etc.).

A victim could deny an abuse suffered in two ways:

1) denying the fact;
2) denying the significance of the fact.

According to one psycho-analytical theory, an impulse is sufficiently unacceptable because it is activated by a defence mechanism, when, according to the sub-conscious judgement of an individual, its expression could result in punishment or revenge on the part of the abuser, or of the internal judge, that is, the moral conscience.

The evaluation of the potential consequences of an impulse reaction does not involve a conscious and intentional process. It is, to the contrary, spontaneous, automatic, and it takes place beyond awareness (White & Gilliland, 1977).

Among the more important defence mechanisms in the study of those situations applying to the so called 'victim in denial', are dismissal and denial.

By **dismissal** is meant a defence mechanism that blocks from the conscience an unbearable internal impulse, and the thoughts, imagination, emotions, and memory associated with it.

When the removal is successful, the impulses removed are completely excluded from the conscience, no sense of conflict is present, neither are any symptoms manifest (White & Gilliland, 1977).

On the other hand, **denial,** means the automatic and involuntary exclusion from awareness of a certain disturbing aspect of the reality, or the inability to recognize its true significance (White & Gilliland, 1977).

The question, however, is far more complex than is proposed here.

The concealing victim

The concealing victim, as opposed to the victim in denial, denies to others what she has suffered but she does not deny it to herself.

In other words, she is aware of having suffered abuse, but she doesn't admit it to others; rather she denies it to others, whoever they may be, thus precluding the possibility of appealing for help (Monzani, 2010, 2011).

The reasons why a subject may knowingly decide not to reveal to third parties her situation of victimization, are by nature more "concrete" when compared with the reasons given by the victim in denial (Monzani, 2010, 2011); usually one deals with more pragmatic reasons, with an objective which is easy and clear to read, without having to resort to psychopathological or psycho-analytical interpretations.

The reasons that could drive a subject to knowingly deny (Read: Concealed) an abuse suffered may be numerous:

a) fear of retaliation on the part of the perpetrator of the abuse or someone acting on his behalf; one thinks of all the cases in which, for example, victims of stalking do not report the abuse suffered because of fear of a possible reaction on the part of the stalker; one thinks, again, of all those cases of domestic violence in which one partner decides to furnish a different version of events (maybe whilst visiting the A & E department) to explain the nature of specific physical injuries.

Reports of previous abuse; such reports may be based on the failure on the part of the victim to report the abuse; from the statistical point of view, in fact, the majority of abuses reported are those carried out by strangers rather than abuses suffered at the hands of those with whom the subject already had a relationship/knowledge before the act; and the stronger and more intimate the relationship, the more difficult it is for the victim to admit their own situation (Monzani, 2011; Gulotta, 1976; Gulotta & Vagaggini, 1981).

b) Financial and logistical problems: Not knowing physically where to go, how to survive financially when one decides to admit finally that one's partner uses violence (Monzani, 2011).

c) The fear of repercussions in the relationship with one's children (e.g. fostering after separation)

The pathway to awareness

To be able to ask for the help they need it is fundamental, as has been seen, that the victim be aware of their status, and the awareness, very often, requires a gradual process of realisation, a path at the end of which a victim will be able to turn to the responsible bodies to ask for the necessary help.

Experience, nevertheless, teaches us that these two situations may also be inverted temporally; it is worth mentioning that, sometimes, the approach itself to particular structures (e.g. Anti-Violence Centres) perhaps only for a first, confused and timid approach, may help the subject to clearly understand the situation of victimization and finally convince her to go through with her action. So, sometimes, the process of realisation could be helped by the very structure to which, theoretically, only subjects that have already followed the pathway to awareness should go.

The pathway to help

The behaviour of the victim is influenced by the society in which she lives, but social behaviour is also influenced by the behaviour of the victim; by that we mean that society, as organized and structured today, does not go looking for victims, but the victims themselves must call attention to the problems that society cannot handle of its own initiative (Eliacheff & Soluez Lariviere, 2008). For this too, current society has a lot to answer for with regard to victims (Ponti, 1995).

Attempting to fill these gaps are organizations (e.g women's movements) that have the job of helping victims to understand their situation and report the abuse, besides supporting them physically, psychologically and financially, etc; all of which can move towards notable social and cultural change. Today, for example, reporting sexual abuse is no longer a matter of shame for the victim (at least, not to the extent that it was at one time), and this is thanks to these associations that have contributed to the understanding of specific problems, and to demolishing certain social and cultural stereotypes which were very common up until a short while ago (Adami, Basaglia, Bimbi & Tola, 2000).

The objective of the pathway to help is to restore the status quo ante, that is, to permit the subject to return to the life she had prior to the situation of victimisation.

There are various possible pathways, depending on the character of the victim, the type of abuse suffered, the kind of relationship she had with the abuser and, not to be underestimated, the type of service that society is able to offer in that particular historic, cultural and financial moment.

There is need to restore the world shattered by the victimisation; a need to put an end to the isolation of the victim and to establish positive contact with her so as to help her to overcome the trauma.

Conclusion

In recent years victims are becoming progressively better organised and have drawn the attention of society and of public opinion, as well as of the institutions, achieving great results.

Now it is necessary to consolidate the above mentioned results, whilst guaranteeing help to the victim by ensuring the presence of a local/national support network (public, private and/or private/social), helping and guiding them by means of the appropriate services, adequately financed and staffed by specialised personnel; otherwise a false expectation is created in the victim (who will wait in vain for the requested help) that will then go disregarded, provoking further suffering and disillusionment – the so-called third victimisation (Monzani, 2011).

In addition, this may stimulate important legislative reforms in order to adapt the legal framework to the changing common conscience (one need think only of the recent reforms regarding sexual assault, or of the laws regarding so-called stalking).

To be able to implement these networks of solidarity and support for the victims of abuse, it is necessary to have an adequate allocation of funds from the government (maybe using part of the assets sequestrated from the convicted perpetrators of the abuse), otherwise the law, even though excellent, risks becoming meaningless, nothing more than a declaration of intent. If that happens, future victims, seeing the failure to provide the requested help to the previous victims, will tend to go back to the practice of not reporting the abuse suffered, thus provoking a regrettable and painful re-victimisation, not to mention an undesirable return to the past.

References

Adami, C., Basaglia, A. & Tola, V. (Eds.). (2002). *Dentro la violenza: cultura, pregiudizi, stereotipi* [Violence in the culture, prejudices, stereotypes]. Milano: Franco Angeli.

Adami, C., Basaglia, A., Bimbi, F. & Tola, V. (Eds.). (2000). *Libertà femminile e violenza sulle donne* [Freedom of women and violence against women]. Milano: Franco Angeli.

Amodio, E., Bondonio, P.V., Carnevali, U., Galli, G., Grevi, V., Pisani, M. & Rubini, L. (1975). *Vittime del delitto e solidarietà sociale* [Victims of crime and social solidarity]. Milano: Giuffrè .

Balloni, A. & Viano, E. (Eds.). (1989). *IV Congresso Mondiale di vittimologia. Atti della giornata bolognese* [IV World Congress of Victimology. Acts of the day in Bologna]. Bologna: Clueb.

De Cataldo Neuburger, L. & Gulotta, G. (1996). *Trattato della menzogna e dell'inganno* [Treaty of lies and deceit]. Milano: Giuffrè.

Eliacheff, C. & Soluez Lariviere, D. (2008). *Il tempo delle vittime* [Time victims]. Milano: Adriano Salani.

Gulotta, G. (1976). *La vittima* [The victim]. Milano: Giuffrè.

Gulotta, G. & Vagaggini, M. (Eds.). (1981). *Dalla parte della vittima* [From part of the victim]. Milano: Giuffrè.

Monzani, M. (2010). *Le vittime in-credibili. Elementi di psicologia forense e della testimonianza* [Victims in-credible. Elements of forensic psychology and witness]. Napoli: Scriptaweb.

Monzani, M. (2011). *Manuale di psicologia giuridica. Elementi di psicologia criminale e vittimologia* [Handbook of forensic psychology. Elements of criminal psychology and victimology]. Padova: Libreria Universitaria.

Monzani, M. (2011b). *Percorsi di criminologia* [Paths of Criminology]. Padova: Libreria Universitaria editore.

Ponti, G. L. (Eds.). (1995). *Tutela della vittima e mediazione penale* [Protection of the victim and mediation]. Milano: Giuffrè.

Saponaro, A. (2004). *Vittimologia. Origini, concetti, tematiche* [Victimology. Origins, concepts, issues]. Milano: Giuffrè.

Testoni, I. (2007). *Cosa nostra e l'uso dell'uomo come cosa. Riflessioni su mafia e de umanizzazione* [Cosa Nostra and the use of man as a thing. Reflections on mafia and de humanization]. Milano: Franco Angeli.

Vezzadini, S. (2006). *La vittima di reato, tra negazione e riconoscimento* [The crime victim, between denial and recognition]. Bologna: Clueb.

Viano, E. (1983). Violence, victimization and social change: a sociocultural and public policy analysis. *International Journal, 8*, 54–79.

Viano, E. (1989). Vittimologia oggi: i principali temi di ricerca e di politica pubblica [Victimology today: major themes of research and public policy]. In A. Balloni & E. Viano (Eds.), *IV Congresso Mondiale di vittimo-logia. Atti della giornata bolognese* [IV World Congress of Victimology. Acts of the day in Bologna] (pp. 125–146). Bologna: Clueb.

White, R. B., & Gilliland, R.M. (1977). *I meccanismi di difesa* [The defense mechanisms]. Roma: Astrolabio.

Part 2. Clinical issues

Women as mothers, lovers, and wives. Inherent representation of role-based violence among psychologists, judiciary system, and social services' network

Caterina Arcidiacono

Introduction

The Family Centre (CPF) of the Health Services of the municipality of Naples (www.centroperlefamiglie.org) carries out counselling and diagnostic activities as well as taking charge of family issues at the request of judiciary authorities. Its area of intervention concerns children with migrant parents, children of mixed couples, and adopted children of foreign origin. In this case, its aim is both to decide what indications must be given to the justice authorities (with reference to the professional knowledge of its experts) and to provide treatment and support aimed at guaranteeing the best for the minor.

The story of Malgorzata and Annamaria is a good example of the complexity of this task and reflexivity as a competence which health workers are asked to provide (Arcidiacono, Ferrari Bravo 2009). In fact, the different national and cultural differences acting in the same country ask us to take into account manifold actors and factors of social interactions, i.e. individuals and their relationships, the contexts where these interactions come into play and, finally, the relationship between context and culture. In fact, when users do not belong to the same cultural background as the health worker and when their life experiences are plainly different from this (e.g. prostitution, marginalization, etc.), the latter must be able to apprehend possible stereotypes and prejudices acting in their relationship with the user. This must be taken into account in particular when social workers and psychologists are asked to write up a legal report on a prosecution. In this case the discussion deals with the meanings of maternal care proposed by the diverse scholars, and it is precisely here that feminist critical psychology comes to the fore as this does not work in a relativist, culturalist dimension but claims its value-related dimension without being either prescriptive or essentialist. If the value attributed to parental care varies across diverse historical periods, what is the vision that must orientate a health worker? What is the best form of motherhood? What type is the most economically stable? Might it be the natural mother bond? Is the maternal or the paternal rule to be in force? These questions underpin the placing and re-placing of children in difficulty in different contexts, which cannot be implicit but are matters of which we must be explicitly aware. Reality, even before showing itself, is always a representation (Mantovani, 2008) constructed by the actors who manage it by virtue of the social power they possess. Therefore, the capacity of health and social personnel for knowing its attitudes and stereotypes and their capacity for reading and understanding those of the users are the underlying competencies for professionals, which good basic training should impart and develop.

The case story

The CPF's (Family Centre) closing time was drawing near when a fax arrived from the juvenile court asking the Centre to guarantee Giuseppe the right to visit Annamaria, his 22-month-old daughter who, due to her father's violent and threatening behaviour towards her mother, is "under protection" in a women's shelter along with the latter who comes from Poland and, according to the enactment, "is taking care of her daughter thoroughly". The case is even more fraught with problems since, at that time, which was around 2000 (in Italy the laws on protection from violent partners or parents have been enacted only during the last decade), the right of a father to see his child was in force, although the law did not then provide any protection whatsoever for victims of violent partners. Thus, the intervention, which we might describe as more as an ad hoc precautionary measure, could never have prevented the father in any way from having contact with his daughter, lest the mother be accused of the removal of a minor child.

What is to be done now? What are the inherent aspects of this case? What is the urgency? The psychologist on call contacts the judge[1] to determine the nature of the enactment, and discovers that the father is not privy to the location of the child and her mother, for "security" reasons. Therefore every encounter must be conducted extremely carefully since there is no enactment whatso-ever by virtue of which the juridical authority can ban a violent father. More-

---

1   This article is dedicated to Paolo Giannini, who was the president of a juvenile court, and to
     Macario Principe, who was a psychologist actively involved in the field of minors. From
     them I acquired the passion and I hope the competence to build up public institutions
     capable of meeting the needs of citizens.

over, this enactment accompanies a request for custody made by the father himself; thus, practitioners cannot take the risk of following an irregular procedure.

The juvenile court requests the CPF (Family Centre) to allow a series of encounters between the child and her father; hence, the psychologist decides to conduct interviews with each parent in order to collect from both of them information about the couple, their relationships with the child, and their future perspectives on how the parental functions will be carried out.

So, the psychologist immediately arranges a preliminary encounter with each parent. However, the mother is reluctant and asks the psychologist to meet her at the institute where she is currently residing in order to provide her with more information about this matter.

The following day the father goes to the CPF to be interviewed; the day after that, the psychologist goes to the convent institute where the woman is staying.

The first encounters

The father, a tall and robust man, arrives punctually. He seems very self-confident, protective and willing to cooperate. The psychologist, who is in charge of the service, is by contrast physically diminutive and therefore has to assert herself in her institutional and professional role. There follows a short sketch in which Giuseppe offers the psychologist his help to open the session room's door, which is locked, by grabbing the keys from the psychologist's hands, proclaiming how accustomed he is to helping women in difficulty.

However, from the psychologist's standpoint, this is a gesture made to place her in the role of a helpless woman, without according her any recognition of her professional position.

During the interview Giuseppe describes Malgorzata and his first encounter with her. According to him, she is a poor woman whom he met in the nightclub where she used to work as a bartender; she is also ill, apparently affected by the radiation from Chernobyl, almost dying and thus unable to take care of her daughter.

The father, a man in his fifties, is the manager of a power utility, married with three daughters. He is claiming custody of his daughter born as the result of an extramarital affair, showing his willingness to provide social solidarity in managing the issues involved in such a "sad case" by taking care of an almost retarded child who is the daughter of such an "unlucky" mother. It seems like a scenario from a nineteenth-century feuilleton.

The following day the encounter between the psychologist, the mother and the child takes place in the Convent Superior's small lounge. Malgorzata is a thirty-two-year-old pale woman with very delicate light-coloured eyes.

Some of the sequences from the first encounter with the mother and her daughter, extrapolated from the psychologist's report, account for the observed interactions:

(From 4 to 5.30 p.m., Institute of hospitality)

"The child is snacking" says the nun, apologising for the delay.

The child enters the room alongside her mum. She is still chewing her small biscuit. She looks at me without making any particular movement, standing on her mother's lap, attached to her body ...

Her mother tells me a story fraught with conflicts and predicaments with her partner; the child moans, cries, flounders, with a growing sense of unease.

When we change the topic she calms down.

She repeats "poop" many times, so her mother stands up, apologising, and leaves the room in order to change her nappy.

When she comes back, the child says "poop stinks".

Her mum replies: "Annamaria, it's fine now"

She hangs around the room, then hides behind the sofa; she walks not far away from us, exploring the room while looking at me and her mother; she comes near and looks at me; her mother carries on with the story... The mother, while talking, shows evident signs of emotion and pain, so the child approaches her with a handkerchief; she sits on her lap and lays her hands under her eyes, with a gesture as to wipe some imagined tears...

The interaction shows the mother as capable of taking care of her daughter's primary needs: she feeds and changes her; she is able to promptly interpret her needs while interacting with her, and so the child seems to interact with her mother accordingly. The competences of the child and the level of interaction with her mother show a child apparently sufficiently mature for her age. What strikes me is the way this child places herself in her mother's arms: it appears entirely glued.

The observation of the mother-child interaction has provided me, as a psychologist, with information about the quality of their relationships and communications. The child, who has been described by her father as well-cared-for since being affected by developmental retardation, is in fact able to emphatically understand her mother and react to her emotional state; she grows restless when the latter shows herself to be angry, and she is a loving rescuer when her mother is in pain – approaching her, for example, with a handkerchief to wipe away her tears. The posture she adopts, in particular when gluing herself to her mother's body, conveys a sense of body continuity, of an archaic two in one, of a still-not-achieved separation.

Malgorzata is a thirty-two-year-old divorced woman and a graduate; in her country she worked as a teacher. She left an eleven-year-old child behind with her mother and came over to Italy on a tourist visa, starting to work as a bartender in a nightclub. Subsequently, she met Giuseppe, an encounter that changed everything: she quit her job and travelled with him before they eventually moved in together.

The first encounter with Malgorzata shows a very different reality from the one described by Giuseppe. Malgorzata seems in good health, trim and able to describe the reasons why she chose to leave Giuseppe and go into hiding. Six months after the baby was born the couple started to come into conflict, a situation exacerbated by their deep cultural differences; subsequently, Giuseppe began to behave violently towards her.

The observation of the interactions allowed an understanding of the good modalities of expression by the child in relation to her mother, highlighting first and foremost her relational skills and the presence of elemental verbal exchanges, which was quite surprising since the child had been described by her father as having been affected by retardation and aphasia.

The observation of mother-child interaction within the nuns' institution provided further information which led the psychologist to look differently at the entire relational framework encompassing the woman, her ex-partner, the services involved and the judicial authority. The young lady encountered in a nightclub while working as a bartender is seen here in her role as a mother. The stereotype of "unfortunate woman who is forced to work at night time" and all the implicit phantoms of "bad mother" related to this are here dissolved when the psychologist observes the diligent care she gives to little Annamaria.

The encounters of the father and his family with the child

The encounters with the child are arranged involving both the mother and the father in a special and particular feature. Since Malgorzata does not want to meet Giuseppe and fears that she will be followed back to the Institute, we arrange to set up the encounters between Giuseppe and his daughter half an hour after Malgorzata arrives at the CPF. In this way there will be no risk of them meeting each other and, at the same time, a health worker will act as a medium in the passage of the child from the mother to the father.

The CPF building has a small corridor at the end of which there are two rooms, one placed on the left and one on the right. Malgorzata and her daughter take a seat in the room on the left, and then accompany the health worker to the playroom on the right; afterwards, towards the time of the encounter with the father, the mother tells Annamaria that she will see her soon and then returns to the room on the left, leaving the door open so that her child can see her and be assured of where she is. Finally, the door of the room where the mother waits is closed and the child remains in the playroom with the health worker awaiting her father.

After the encounter, once the father is gone, the child remains in the Family Centre with her mother for another quarter of an hour in order to ensure that her father has long gone. Sometimes, after an encounter, when Malgorzata and her daughter have doubts about their safety, they are accompanied to the institute by a CPF trainer health worker.

Within this rigid frame, the encounters take place first only between Annamaria and her father, and then, at the explicit request of the latter, between his wife and/or sons as well.

Annamaria sits on her father's lap looking at him and sometimes smiling. However, when her father takes her on his lap her body remains distant, exhibiting nothing like the adhesion and utter possessiveness shown in the interaction with the maternal body.

The child, who is usually silent during the encounters, once in the car with her mother tells her about them. However, the child speaks neither with her father nor with his family nor, at least initially, with any of the strangers who try to interact with her. She starts speaking only with one of her brothers, in a non-verbal manner, by showing glee.

After a while she begins to play. Her favourite game with Giuseppe and the health worker consists in throwing a ball back and forth, a sort of cotton reel game which shows the unconscious aspects of the approaching and leaving. The majority of times she herself ends the interviews by putting on her small raincoat and moving towards her stroller in which she tries to curl up.

Meanwhile the interviews between the psychologist and both the parents and Giuseppe's wife and sons continue.

A complex picture within a stable frame

As the encounters proceed, a complex scenario starts to take shape. Everyone tells their own version of the story: Giuseppe remarks that Malgorzata is unable to care for the child, unlike his wife who has brought up three healthy and strong children; hence he lays claim to the custody of his daughter even though she is the result of an extramarital affair.

Giuseppe's view

Giuseppe tells the psychologist how much he was in love with the beautiful Malgorzata; he went along with her to Poland to meet her family, showing photos of her house and her first daughter standing beside him in the bedroom. He says that, in order to obtain an Italian residency permit for her, he made her marry one of his friends and afterwards let her stay in his house with his wife and children, before eventually renting a flat in the San Marcellino neighbourhood where she could live in a dignified way while taking care of her daughter. But all of this has been "unworthily" rejected by Malgorzata.

Now he is waiting for the juvenile court to give him and his wife custody of his daughter, considering how unreasonably her natural mother has behaved in rejecting his attempts to take care of her and the child.

A clash between different cultural matrices starts to take shape. The middle-aged man who has an extramarital affair with a young woman regards himself as adequate and in the right since he provides for his lover and her daughter while at the same time "respecting" his legitimate wife and family. It is the foreigner who ought to be thankful for all this attention; hence she should reciprocate by being faithful and respectful (on this account she is not expected to go out on her own, not even shopping; it is he who provides for her, so the mother of his child must show seriousness and respect). The conflict arises as Malgorzata does not accept the requirement to live as a recluse, renouncing any social and cultural life.

Adelina's perspective

Let us now examine how Adelina, Giuseppe's wife, describes the situation and her feelings. Adelina is a woman in her fifties, as big and robust as her husband. She neither blames him nor seems to harbour any grudge. "He always made sure we lacked nothing, he has always been a zealous father ready to meet his children's needs" she says. Her role as a wife has never been called into question and her husband has never intended to abandon her, which is why she has always been willing to take care of the child and bring her up within the bosom of her family just as she did with the others (her natural sons). Being supportive of her husband, she lays claim to the child, of whom she has become fond.

The mother, Malgorzata, as one might expect, is unwilling to accept the restrictions imposed by her ex-partner or to give up her baby.

The observation of the context (Arcidiacono, 2009) and the reciprocal interactions provided information on inter-relationships that have confirmed the relational jigsaw puzzle which emerged from the interviews, and mainly from the encounters between the father and his child. When Adelina, Giuseppe's wife, arrives at the CPF, she immediately changes the child, making her wear a different dress and justifying the need for her to wear a particularly fine dress. Before leaving, she undresses the child and puts the dress away in readiness for the next encounter. The inherent violence of this act is not recognized by the protagonists in this play, so the psychologist feels forced to take note of it although she cannot express her emotions in words.

At the same time the psychologist notices that Adelina has brought a chest key with which Annamaria particularly used to enjoy playing; with this gesture, Adelina is trying to reconnect strings that had been cut, and she is using shared objects which carry a sense of bonding and continuity at the same time. However, what strikes the psychologist is the fact that even the food is changed regularly.

Here the bond rule seems to be inscribed in a belonging framework. Usually, every encounter at the CPF took place during lunch time; therefore the participants were all concerned that Annamaria should not skip her lunch. Her mother used to bring a banana with a fruit juice and /or a yogurt. However, if the child was eating the banana this would be replaced with biscuits, for example; or, perhaps, on another occasion the fruit juice she was drinking would be described as "not good" and would be replaced with another one. Clothes and food seem here to convey the rules of belonging. Giuseppe, the householder, has a baby – Annamaria – and for this to be accepted it must be inscribed within the family heritage. Clothes and food assume distinction-based values with exclusion-based characteristics distinguishing them from everything that is not placed within the family.

The institutional legal frame

Let us now consider the situation from an institutional standpoint. Annamaria was born in Italy to an Italian father and a Polish mother who is at risk of losing her residency permit. No juvenile court would ever give custody of an Italian child to a clandestine migrant mother instead of her father whose financial condition is solid and who has a stable family life.

The services in charge of the case show themselves to be not critical when faced with prejudices of alleged inadequacy, which are put forward by the spouses, attributed to Malgorzata. Therefore, the state of affairs seems complex and difficult to manage. The request sent to the CPF initially asks practitioners only to guarantee the encounters between the father and his child and then to report what has happened in them to the judicial authority.

Afterwards it will be asked to judge the ability of the mother to take care of her child in order to decide whether or not the mother lacks parental skills and, thus, whether custody of the child should be awarded to her father. The judicial case is completely focused on the father's claim to the daughter given the alleged inadequacy of the maternal care.

The CPF's intervention and its rationale

Being charged with responsibility for the case of a minor child of an Italian father and a mother on the brink of becoming a clandestine migrant, the CPF has tried to determine the best socially supportive measures to provide by attempting to view the case from a global perspective. In particular, the health workers took into account the future of the child, the meaning of maternal care, and basically what kind of intervention strategies might best be employed. In that sense, the guideline for the intervention followed what Prilleltensky holds to be the affirmation of rights and justice (Nelson & Prilleltensky, 2005; Prilleltensky, Dokecki, Frieden & Wang, 2007). Thus, the first step seemed to have been taken towards respecting the rights of a clandestine migrant mother with reference to those of her Italian daughter who is subject to different legislation. Therefore, the first thing was to provide her with a residency permit and help her find a job which would allow her to keep the child.

One year after the marriage, Giuseppe's friend, who volunteered to marry Malgorzata, is supposed to confirm to the foreigner office that the marriage condition is unchanged, but he has said that he will not do so. It seems plain that Giuseppe has interceded with him in this matter. Malgorzata therefore appears to have no chance of finding a job and seems likely to be denied custody of her child as a consequence. No judge, indeed, according to the personnel of the CPF, would ever give custody of an Italian child to a clandestine migrant Polish mother.

So, the CPF was active in helping Malgorzata with her administrative obligations: her declaration of residence and request for residency permission; here, too, the bureaucratic procedure is not smooth.

As regards the request to monitor the encounters between Annamaria and her father, these proceed regularly along with the interviews with Malgorzata, Giuseppe, his wife, and his children over and above the observations of the reciprocal interactions made during the encounters with the child. The encounters continue for three months until Malgorzata and her daughter move to another region, as she has found a good opportunity to work as a caretaker in a family that is willing to let her stay there together with her daughter.

Therefore, being aware of the socially vulnerable situation of Malgorzata, it was decided to continue providing distance supportive activities. First, Malgorzata was asked to provide the judge with her new address and the latter built up contacts with the Venetian judicial authorities who arranged a series of encounters between the child and her father at weekends. The enactment involved local social services as well, since it was at their premises that the father would pick up and drop off the child.

Initially the psychologist of the CPF kept in touch with Malgorzata through weekly phone encounters. Subsequently, Malgorzata was available for telephone conversations on Monday mornings in order to report how the relationship between father and daughter was progressing, while awaiting a definitive enactment for the custody of the latter. Malgorzata seemed to have withdrawn into a depressive state, so the psychologist wanted the CPF to represent an open space for her, a sort of active communication channel.

Meanwhile, the CPF personnel built up the encounters between the child and her father.

The interaction between the child and her father seems to have been recreationally/instrumentally characterised although, even in the last case, it seems emotionally connoted and adequate for her age. Through analyses of the observations it was possible to draw the conclusion that the child has good relational and communicative skills and is able to emotionally recognise what is going on with her parents and consequently interact with their emotions; she also appears to be able to express her needs and to show curiosity, although she exhibits a certain reluctance when in the presence of other adults.

In particular, only repeated observations in different relational contexts allow practitioners to understand the social interactions of a child who is observed in a relational context marked by repeated separations.

In conclusion, there seemed to be good interaction and communication between mother and child, contrary to the claims of Giuseppe and his wife.

This work enabled the deciphering of implicit meanings, stereotypes and prejudices which the institutional system had wrongly attributed to the maternal care. In fact, each service with which Malgorzata has been in touch has read the case in a different way, particularly with reference to the diverse backgrounds of the health workers involved. In that sense, it is worth noting that when Malgorzata moved to Treviso the social workers mistakenly believed her to be "indifferent" because of her reluctance to show pain when separating from her child every time she had to meet her father. However, since the psychologist from the CPF had established a trusting relationship with this woman, by supporting her when the child was with her father and when his family prevented her from having contact with her daughter, the continuity and constancy of the support for Malgorzata allowed her to piece together different information to eventually obtain a constituent framework.

In this case, the attempt to explicate the complex relational dynamic at family and inter-institutional levels, along with the material gathered through the observations, allowed practitioners to make a careful examination of the complex system of relationships between professional and non-professional figures, finally motivating the judge to confirm that custody of the child should be given to her mother. The psychoanalytically-oriented observation (Boursier,

2010) has been the key tool for exploring the relationships between the child and her natural mother, father, brothers and prospective foster mother.

The inter-institutional competence and the clinical and developmentally-oriented education of the health workers allowed them to set up an intervention in which social dimensions are intertwined with complex and deeply social as well as emotionally-affectively characterized inter-relational dynamics related to the maternal and feminine identity of the two women and "mothers" in question, as well as the paternal-marital identity of the man.

Moreover, it is worth noting the effect of stereotypes and prejudices resulting from the fact that the protagonists in this case belonged to different cultures. As described in "La torre di Babele" by Amati-Mehler et al,(1990), the knowledge of linguistic issues usually carried by children who have grown up in bilingual contexts (Italian, Polish, Neapolitan in the case in question) has allowed them to overcome the "alleged" and "selfish" paternal concerns.

This work was aimed at mediating the encounter between people of different cultures with reference to both the family relationships and the institutional procedures. These are differences, which can be ascribed not only to diverse national realities but also in relation to the various ways of valuing the man-woman relationship in general.

Giuseppe, after being away with his young lover for varying lengths of time, has eventually come back home.

His wife is willing to accept his daughter, who was born of an extra-marital affair, as long as the marital tie is not cut off. This decision seems to be in line with widespread contemporary practices and social customs of emarginated sub-cultural groups.

Malgorzata is placed, instead, in a more "emancipated" dimension: she is a woman who does not bother to have an extramarital affair – she claims her right to self-autonomy and the recognition of her maternal role.

Malgorzata used to live in Giuseppe's family home along with his wife and children, the one she called "granpa's house". And it was precisely there that a clash with Adelina, symbol of reciprocal relationships and feelings, occurred. According to the story, Malgorzata was so depressed that Adelina had not hesitated to take her into her house along with her child, and the latter had displayed no objection to living in Giuseppe's marital home along with his wife and children. However, Malgorzata claimed her maternal role in order to be respected. Instead, Adelina, who was older and more "competent" than her, would insist on being the only one to take care of the whole family by deciding what was best for everybody. So, when Annamaria once showed the symptoms of a prolonged and alarming constipation, Adelina decided to proceed with the use of enemas. This decision met with opposition from Malgorzata who did not see the need for them. Within this conflict, Giuseppe sided with his wife, who "had brought up his children and his entire family", by suggesting that Malgorzata should have given Adelina credit for her competence. The clash between maternal competencies represented a real *casus belli*. Since then, it was, in fact, decided that Annamaria and her mother should have lived elsewhere. Malgorzata, being aware of her precarious situation and her dependence on Giuseppe, probably consented to live in his house with his wife, and the latter accepted the situation while grinning and bearing it, although she had the satisfaction of keeping her husband in the marital home and being recognized for her maternal and caring competencies in respect of the entire family. However, conflict had been avoided as long as Malgorzata was deemed to be Giuseppe's friend's wife. Faced with the denial of her maternal competencies in the context of her refusal to allow hygienic practices she deemed to be intrusive for her child, she rose up in rebellion.

By reading Giuseppe's and his wife's behaviour through the lenses of a patriarchal culture, the situation becomes more comprehensible: after all, by taking up his natural child the father shows his reluctance to abandon her while seeking to avoid jeopardising his legitimate family's bonds at the same time. In this traditional scenario, the young lover belonging to a social subculture is not supposed to claim any rights; rather, she should gratefully accept the help offered to her daughter who was born of an extramarital affair. This explains Giuseppe's incredulity at Malgorzata's decision to work and care for her daughter at the same time.

Observation, as a working tool, allowed the personnel to walk through a field made by various cultures with reference to different values while trying to keep their value autonomy without overruling the others'.

The observation has turned out to be an experience, which has helped the practitioners to understand relational processes and open up the possibility for the institutional interventions to reflect upon them *a posteriori*.

The encounters between daughter and father, which were initially requested by the juvenile court, have taken place at a concrete level at the CPF premises where the subjects involved have, in fact, interacted in a dimension of reality. However, the mediation worked at a further level – the inter-subjective dimension – into which the feelings, emotions, and representations of the Other flow and also where the health personnel can work with the Other through their own emotions, feelings, intentions and abilities.

The institutional intervention carried out on behalf of Annamaria, a 22-month-old child, and her interaction with her Polish mother and her Neapolitan father, who is happily married with three children although in love with the young foreigner, is emblematic of the stereotypes attributed to mother-daughter relationships and social representations of adequate maternal care.

Both the judge and the CPF were aware of the violent dimension of coercion inherent in the obligation of "soberness" imposed on Malgorzata (do not go out, do not speak to anybody). We were also aware of the depressive state that was troubling this woman, although her response seemed to us quite understandable given the circumstances; in that sense, we knew how much a definition of Malgorzata's behaviour expressed in a pathological manner might preclude the decision to award her custody of the child. Finally, we were aware of the extent of institutional normative power and its abusive effect on human bonds. On these grounds, the Monday phone calls with Malgorzata have been continuing for over a year, making, in fact, the CPF Malgorzata's and Annamaria's Italian local support and family at large.

References

Amati-Mehler, J., Argentieri, & Canestri, J. (1993). *The Babel of the Unconscious: Mother Tongue and Foreign Tongues in the Analytic Dimension.* International Universities PressInc, (IT, ed. 1990).

Arcidiacono, C. (1996). *Identità femminile e psicoanalisi. Da donna a donna: Alla ricerca del senso di sé.* Milano: FrancoAngeli.

Arcidiacono, C., & Ferrari Bravo G. (2009). *Legami resistenti. Invio regolamentato e famiglie in difficoltà.* FrancoAngeli: Milano.

Arcidiacono, C. (2009). *Riflessività, processualità, situatività: parole chiave della ricerca-azione.* In: Ricerche di psicologia, numero speciale a cura di F.P. Colucci, (pp.113-126) Vol XXXI, n.3-4.

Boursier, V. (2010). *Sentire con gli occhi, Note sull'osservazione del bambino in psicoanalisi tra formazione, clinica e ricerca.* FrancoAngeli: Milano.

Chodorow, N. (1978). *The reproduction of mothering: psychoanalysis and sociology of gender.* Berkeley, Los Angeles: University of California Press.

Ferraro, F., & Nunziante Cesàro A. (1985) *Lo spazio cavo e il corpo saturato.* FrancoAngeli, Milano.

Mantovani, G. (2008). (ed.) *Intercultura e mediazione.* Roma, Carocci.

Nelson, G., & Prilleltensky, I. (Eds.) (2005). *Community psychology: In pursuit of liberation and well-being.* New York, NY: Palgrave MacMillan.

Prilleltensky, I., Dokecki, P., Frieden, G. & Wang,V. O. (2007). Counseling for Wellness and Justice: Foundations and Ethical Dilemmas in: (E. Aldarondo, ed.) *Advancing Social Justice Through Clinical Practice.* Stratford Books, United Kingdom.

From the maternal to the Self: psychodrama for the promotion of female agency in overcoming the internalized victimary role

Ines Testoni, Maria Silvia Guglielmin, Ingrid Pogliani,
Daniela Di Lucia Sposito, Gabriela Dima, Michael Wieser,
Sibylla Verdi, Alessandra Armenti

Introduction

In this chapter we consider the problem of motherhood's psychological role with respect to their daughters that are victims of domestic violence. We assume the gender perspective which views this question as a psychosocial problem determined by cultural causes. In spite of the fact that cultural explanations of gender violence are contested because they are used to excuse individual actions, we assume the perspective of Messing and Adelman (Messing, Adelman & Durfee, 2012; Adelman, Haldane & Wies, 2012) in whose opinion, the contestation of this idea can be found in the strategies of defense of gender violence linked to the re-traditionalization of family. We admit that this cultural perspective has been used to defend or excuse gender violence and is therefore seen as a barrier to the elimination of gender violence, but, in concurrence with the authors, we equally consider how culture may also be mobilized strategically as a resource in the struggle against gender violence. From this perspective, we think that any social program aimed at changing the actual situation must firstly modify the cultural background and related stereotypes, since culture is often responsible for *how* the problem of violence against women is viewed and addressed. In particular, we believe that domestic violence results from the traditionalist maintenance and/or restoration of separation between natural and social tasks that are divided between males and females. Indeed, the social versus the household's gender division of labor, which is the fundamental aspect of public-private gendered split, determines gender wage gaps resulting from a comparative advantage of men over women in work outside the family (Burker & Feiner, 2004; Beneira,

1979), in the process thereby making men inept in family relationships and women in social ones. The reinforcement of the female expectation of getting married and becoming a mother, which again characterizes most women even in the Western contemporary crisis, has a huge influence on women's socialization and occupational choices. To this effect, the preferences for jobs that are more readily available to women are conservative ones, such as teaching, nursing, and secretarial work.

Gender segregation in the labor market and the glass ceiling are the result of cultural variables which determine the inferior status of women and, as a consequence, their subordination both in intimate and social relationships. Indeed, gender inequality is embedded within the social hierarchy, thus affecting how women and men are perceived in power management, and in everyday relationships, both social and domestic. Moreover, domestic labor plays an important role in creating and maintaining women's subordinate status (Barker, 2003; Ridgeway, 2001) since those skills that are culturally required in female domestic activities, of which care-giving and motherhood are among the most important, are in contrast with the skills of the masculine Homo Oeconomicus Model, according to which men must organize their chosen pursuits in a rational life plan, allowing them to decide which of their desires are most urgent and how they might more efficiently achieve them (Walker, 1998).

Mother blaming and cultural double bind

In every culture, motherhood is often associated with female realization; women are still under severe pressure to become a mother and to bear children, therefore they accept the view that childbearing is a natural and necessary part of their life. Consequently this leads to the idealization of mothering as an extension of emphasized femininity and thus women who are socially employed feel guilty or are accused of being selfish when they pursue goals that are different from the primary duty of motherhood. Such pressure for women to bear children does not derive merely from personal view points, but mostly from cultural symbolism, which is transferred through the mother-daughter relationship, and thereby influencing their individual attitudes.

The confinement of women within close relationships or primary socialization produces their feeling of inferiority through a particular form of victim blaming: "mother blaming." This issue is addressed here as one expression of the mother's responsibility for the daughter's experience of domestic violence, a discussion which will be later differentiated from the blaming which characterizes the sexist culture.

Mother blaming is the result of the females relegation to the domestic sphere, and it is conditioned by the primary responsibility of mothers for the emotional and moral development of the children. Compared with fathers, mothers are in fact more involved with the responsibility for daily childcare, which exposes them to a wider range of disagreements and tension with their children. In addition to the above mentioned mother blaming, there is also a related image of "bad mothers" that corresponds to the social representation of the woman's inefficacy in her most important duty in life: which is to ensure the healthy and happy growth of her children. As Chodorow shows (1978, 1989), there is a tendency for two types of attitudes towards mothers in modern society, which are either blaming or idealizing. The first consists in the all-powerful mother belief ("Good Mother Myths" [GMM] or "so-called good-enough mother"), the second is the "guilty mother" who causes mental illness ("Bad Mother Myths" [BMM]). The social propensity to explain negative outcomes for children by focusing on the failures of mother-hood considers mothers too close or too distant, too strict or too permissive, unable to set clear enough boundaries or to guarantee effective empathy, love and positive affections. The topics of the good/bad mother are central to the psychological description of mother-child relationships. In psychoanalytical literature, the bad mother myths have been applied from the perspective of object relations and attachment theories, which consider psychological sufferance and pathologies as resulting both from primary breakdowns in the mother relationship and then from separation anxiety (Suttie, 1988). Although Western culture glorifies the idea of motherhood through GMM, a severe denigration of individual and real mothers permeates culture and academic studies, which evoke BMM (Ladd-Taylor & Umansky, 1998). Mothers have been blamed for every kind of problem, hence also the symbol of the "refrigerator mother" causing autism (Fitzpatrick, 2009) and anorexia (Vander Ven & Vander Ven, 2003). In spite of the fact that contemporary culture lives in the era of mind-brain identity, and that the more neuro-sciences evolve, the less interest there is in psychological causes of mental diseases one can still perceive the constant creation of new forms of mother blaming for their child's diseases (Blum, 2007). In this area, determined by both the economic crisis and the political erosion of the welfare state's social services, the quickest strategy to overload mother roles with responsibilities and tasks, aimed at replacing the lack of social care and education, is to stop the dynamics of female empowering and bring women into the domination of conservative cultures ("anti-feminist backlash") (Backlash, 1991).

The psychological culture of mother blaming both provokes self-doubt among mothers and sanctions them to stay at home rather than trying to find a social space.

In fact, when inter-connected with changing ideas about real social female roles, blaming mothers for giving their children too much or not enough attention, is a massive double bind, in that women are fitted into a situation in which any successful response actually results in a failed response, so that whatever the solution, the mother is automatically wrong. Thus, as in every paradoxical relationship, women cannot confront the inherent dilemma of motherhood and therefore cannot resolve or opt out of the situation, because she is not sufficiently aware of the fact that the more sexist the culture, the more numerous the forms of pre-proscriptions mother blaming creates for what she should be. Moreover, since double binds are often utilized as a form of social control without open coercion (Bateson, 1972), the contradiction makes it difficult for women to respond/react or resist, and thus they themselves are often the first factor of conservative restoration. This is our starting point: the average woman is not involved in promoting gender consciousness, and is unaware of the double bind in which they are caught up in. As victims of sexist social power, whose hegemonic culture produces a double bind aimed at maintaining its dominant roles, women reproduce their subjugation. GMM may be considered as the opposite of the masculine *Homo Oeconomicus* Model. In fact, a so-called "good-enough" mother is not allowed to be rational, selfish and interested primarily in her own needs. A good mother, for the sake of her offspring, must also know how to live with "homo oeconomicus" and how to bear with him, in order to keep the balance in the family (Ferber & Nelson, 2003; Persky, 1995). The mother-daughter relationship may be an important contributing factor in the continued perpetuation of these dynamics, whereby in conservative cultures, mothers teach daughters to be patient and devoted to the needs of her husband and children. In this kind of relationship, the assumption of the victim role may be passed down from mother to daughter.

Empower Project and the research

The most important problem connected to the maintenance and return of conservative culture and thus the re-establishment of female subordination revolves around the preservation of gender based violence, and in particular of domestic violence (Laidler & Mann, 2008).

    In accordance with Lawler's opinion (Lawler, 2000) which shows how, in Western culture, women have been held responsible for child rearing and how their adherence to the so-called "good-enough mother," model, which results from specific cultural prescriptions, is co-responsible for the continuation of female subordination, we will consider a specific dimension of the problem in this contribution. If the mother and daughter discourse is particularly important because, as Lawler affirms, it may generate a real social inter-generational change, then it is also true that this relationship, as a product of gendered social and political dynamics, is actually a cause of the historical transmission of female subjugation through traditionalist values. From this perspective, we can affirm that the unattainable standards represented by the GGM and BMM, deriving from the societal expectations for women to be "good mothers," is a factor causing mothers' sufferance (Villani & Ryan, 1997) with the consequential effects of both self-denial and the subsequent unconscious retaliation against the children, and in particular against the daughter.

"Empower" is part of the European Daphne III Project (EEDP) which has considered this problematic issue. Its first aim is to use psychodrama and socio drama to study and modify the function of the mothers' role for women dealing with violence. It involves helping female victims of violence become aware of the history of their condition and of how it leads to the unconscious perpetuation of the cycle of subjugation from mothers to daughters. Empower has helped these women achieve resilience and effective self-determination by rising above the limits imposed by intergenerational relationships. The goal of empowering and improving coping strategies towards greater resilience has been accomplished by means of psychodramatic techniques, which teach women how the dynamics of their role and position in society have determined their own lives. The aim has been to provide victims with an environment for psychological development, and to offer special attention to the roles they have internalized that were passed down by the mother.

Psychodrama is a methodology that uses action methods, sociometry, role playing, and group dynamics to facilitate constructive change in the lives of the participants. Based on the theories and methodology of Jacob L. Moreno, psychodrama can be found in mental health programs, business, and education (Moreno, 1953, 1972). By closely approximating life situations in a structured setting, the participant may recreate and enact scenes in a way that both allows insight into, and an opportunity to practice new life skills. In psycho-drama, the client (or protagonist) focuses on a specific situation to be enacted. Other members of the group act as auxiliaries, supporting the protagonist in his or her work, by taking the parts or roles of significant others in the scene. The trained director helps to recreate scenes which might otherwise not be possible. The psychodrama then becomes an opportunity to practice new and more appropriate behaviors, and evaluate their effectiveness within the supportive atmosphere of the group.

Through psychodrama, Empower deals with violence that arises from the status of being a woman, while through the ecological matrix counseling component, we take care of the relational space in which women interact. The project planned for all six participating countries (Italy, Albania, Austria, Bulgaria, Portugal and Romania), to have two groups: one group led only by social workers through support counseling and the other group which in addition to this support offered psychodrama. This methodology involved the participation in a psychodrama group for six months for a total of 25 sessions of two hours each. The only exception was Albania where the groups taking part in the psychodrama participated in four marathon session of three days.

The decision to dedicate a qualitative space to EPDP research stems from this theoretical background and from the consequent need to comply with a bottom-up hermeneutics matrix that is able to offer a representation that adheres to the reality of the problem experienced by victims. This type of methodology is particularly appreciated by feminist and Gender Studies approaches, which highlight how it is possible to transform the narration into "agency," which is already a first step towards change brought about by a realization or awareness. To conduct research following a cultural perspective does not therefore mean to expect and claim to capture the world as it actually is in reality, but to access reality through the mediating lens of artefacts (Zucchermaglio, 2002). In this area of studies, EPDP is aimed at highlighting one of the most important emotional aspects experienced by victims: unmanaged inner aggression. The guideline was to consider how psycho-drama helps to manage aggression, considered on the one hand as violence and on the other hand as the primary subjective emotion. The hypothesis is that the psychodramatic work allows the victims to deal with the violence experienced, in order to transform internalized aggression into an impetus for the liberation from oppression. To detect this possible effect produced by psychodramatic techniques, a qualitative analysis was designed and based on a specific assessment, as follows: protocols with open-ended questions containing personal data about the family of origin, incidents, episodes of violence, social atom relationships and monthly reports sent by the psychodramatists. The construction of the protocol involved the collaboration between specialized anti-violence centres and Associations of Classical Morenian psychodramatists: in Italy, the Anti-violence centre in the municipality of Rovigo; in Albania, Refleksione; in Austria, Mädchenzentrum Klagenfurt-Caritas Carinthia; in Bulgaria, the Bulgarian society for psychodrama and group therapy – The Nadia Centre Foundation; in Portugal, Societade Portuguesa de Psycho drama SPP – Umar; in Romania, the Romanian Association of Classical Psychodrama – Home of hope.[1]

The target group and the textual reports

Subjects were identified from a group of 57 women; and the text of 52 reports formed the core materials for the qualitative analysis. In particular, we

1   We would like to extend our thanks to the following psychodramatists: Nicoletta Gola, Angela, Chiavassa, Luciana Basilicò (Italy), Gabriela Dima, Carmen Patrascu (Romania), Karin Leitgeb, Elisabeth Mairitsch, Daniela Trattnigg, (Austria) Maria Gorinova, Teo-dora Pencheva (Bulgaria), Joào Teixera de Sousa, and José Luis Mesquita (Portugal).

examined certain forms of representations emerging from the psychodramatic activities which characterize the experience of anger and aggression.

The characteristics of the total group of victims attending the psychodrama sessions are described in Table 1. The complete assessment developed for the qualitative analysis has been planned in the following way: Monthly reports compiled by the psychodramatists containing the transcripts of the psychodrama sessions; social and family atoms completed by the female participants; and forms to be filled out by the social workers, in order to collect the victims personal data as well as information pertaining to their family life and to episodes of violence.

Country	N	Group		Age (years)			Education (years)	
		PG	EG	Range	M	SD	M	SD
Italy	14	8	6	26-58	38.64	9.37	13.21	3.86
Austria	33	19	14	16-68	41.15	12.78	12.13	3.26
Bulgaria	21	9	12	22-66	39.71	12.02	14.33	2.49
Portugal	17	7	10	24-68	46.4	12.72	7.9	3.26
Romania	33	15	18	19-62	33.18	9.15	11.48	3.55
Albania	18	12	6	15-24	20	3.38	7.38	3.10
Total	136	70	66	15-68	36,6	12,95	11.28	3.98

Table 1. Socio-demographic data of women victim of violence in Empower Project

In this particular contribution, the qualitative analysis is considered as an inherent part of the monthly reports. Each report was a maximum of 250 words long and had to be completed during the first psychodrama session, as well as at every first monthly psychodrama session and at the final group session. The report had to contain the following items: the name of the women attending the psychodramatic sessions; the meetings held in the previous month; the aspects represented by the family figures (mother, father, brothers/sisters, partner/husband & children); the topic to be addressed in the session; the most significant moment of the session; the most meaningful questions that the psychodramatist asked during the session; and when possible, the mother-daughter relationship. Every report was written by the psychodramatists in English and sent to the qualitative analysis team. Between November 2011 and July 2012, a total of 52 monthly reports were sent by all the Countries involved (see Table 2). Romania and Bulgaria had a second group, whose sessions began in February 2012. In Albania, the Italian psychodramatists worked with the help of a translator and the meetings took place over two weekends in the form of marathon psychodramatic sessions.

Country	Nr. authors of the reports	N. reports	Words	Range time	When
Italy	2	7	1750	January 2012- July 2012	Monthly
Austria	3	15	3750	Group 1: December 2011- April 2012 Group 2: December 2011- May 2012 Group 3: December 2011- May 2012	Monthly
Bulgaria	2	10	2500	Group 1: December 2011- March 2012 Group 2: April 2012- July 2012	Monthly
Portugal	1	8	2000	December 2012-July 2012	Monthly
Romania	2	8	2000	Group 1: November 2011-February 2012 Group 2: February 2012-February 2012	Monthly
Albania	2	4	1000	November-December 2011	1 every 2 weeks
Total	12	52	13.000		

Table 2. Description of text documentation

Each group took part in 25 sessions of psychodrama, and each session was two hours long. In Albania, four intensive meetings were organized, each of which lasted three days, since it was not possible to hold standard sittings. In these Albanian sessions, there were two groups that had two sessions lasting 3 hours over a period of 3 days.

The sessions were usually divided into the same four parts for each of the participating countries: greeting the women in the group and getting an update on their experiences with respect to the previous week or the period since the last meeting; doing a warm-up using the topics suggested by the group leaders, followed by psychodramatic activities; psychodramatic group or protagonist work; and final participation by everyone through sharing emotions, thoughts and memories that were stimulated during the meeting. The themes agreed on included: me and we; me, we and others; my, our family stories; work on specific topics like security, fear, guilt and assertiveness; cultural analyses; and our power.

The qualitative analysis

EPDP processed the reports using Atlas.ti, which is a powerful software that is very useful in carrying out the qualitative analysis of text (Muhr, 1991) and offering support to the researcher during the work. The process provides a comprehensive overview of the research, meanwhile organizing all the primary documents and identifying the common denominating characteristic. This in turn allows the visual connection of selected texts and codes through the logical and consistent use of diagrams. Data segments, or units, are then organized into a bottom-up system, meaning a system that is predominantly derived from the data. The researcher defines those categories which identify conceptual similarities and then expresses the patterns in the text. These categories are flexible and may be modified during the analysis, in order to produce an output along the lines of a higher-order syntheses. These relate to the substantive theories implied and are presented in a descriptive format. Data is then broken down. The descriptions form the basis of the analysis, and the analysis forms the basis for further descriptions. In this way, theories and concepts are created by classifying the data and vice-versa. Descriptions of meaning provide the basis for each process of analysis. This process is led by the researchers, who are aware of the latent bias of their work, which may derive from their preconceived ideas. The data in the text is processed in the following order: recognition of the Units of Analysis (UA); assignment of the UA to categories or classes; identification of formal connections between them; patterns identified; identification of associations between categories and output consisting in the production of graphs to describe the logical relationships between those concepts and categories as identified by the researcher. EPDP has adopted a cyclical and bi-phasic procedure. The first phase is bottom-up and consists in reading the text, followed by the construction of categories (words or short sentences) taken from the actual wording of the text, and again, reading. The second phase is top-down, since it infers the system codes from key concepts of already existent theories. This cycle continues until a system of codes is able to adequately capture the meaning of the texts with respect to the objectives of the research. EPDP has classified and encoded all the contingencies and distinctive features in accordance with the key-concept of psychodrama and agency/empower theories.

After the first phase of encoding, the creation of networks and graphs follows in order to produce the map and to organize the principal topics and their logical relationships. This is done by means of a graphic apparatus which is able to organize the data and to view it spatially. The networks are thus configured as graphic representations. These relationships reciprocally connect the nodes according to a hierarchical or symmetrical order and are displayed through certain specific symbols (see Figure 1).

Relationship	Symbols	Formal Attributes
It is related to/with	= =	Symmetrical
It is part of	[]	Transitive
It is cause of	=>	Transitive
Contradicts	<>	Symmetrical
It is a...	Isa	Transitive
It is owned by	*}	Asymmetric

Figure 1. Symbols description used in Atlas.ti graphs

Discussion on the analysis of the texts

In Albania there were two separate groups of women. The psychodramatists who led the sessions were from Italy and they worked with a translator. Thus for logistical reasons, in Albania we held four "intensive" psychodramatic sessions over two weekends. From Albania we received four reports. Both groups were made up of six women. The participants in the first group were all residents of a protected community for women who have been victims of violence, while the participants in the second group had turned to an anti-violence centre called Refleksione, although they did not reside in the community. In Albania (see Table 1), the psychodramatists asked the participants to pick an image to represent them. The figure chosen was that of a mother as well as the image of a pregnant woman. The common element shared by all the group members was the recollection of their own mother, unable to recognize their real needs. During the psychodrama sessions these needs emerged as the need to feel supported – and to start their lives afresh.

Austria had three groups of psychodrama and a total of 19 participants. Austria submitted a total of 15 monthly reports describing the psychodrama sessions of the three groups (see Table 2). The mother's role was addressed in several sessions which were geared towards taking care of themselves and others. The resulting representations were complex as they include ambivalent features between love and denial. The psychodramatic work was focused on enabling women to become aware of what was missing from their lives and the negativity experienced in order to enable them to find resources to give themselves what they need and that the mother was not able to provide. From this starting point the women have changed their own representation of themselves as mothers.

Bulgaria set up two groups of psychodrama for a total of 10 monthly reports. (see Table 2). The maternal representations were investigated by the psychodramatists through a compilation and a subsequent "actioning" out of family atoms, through activities about the family roles and thoughts about episodes of life. The relationship with the mother emerges categorized by the absence of support and understanding. The women say that they have been taught victim roles and to remain "quietly at home."

In Portugal there were seven women who attended the psychodrama group. The Portuguese psychodramatists submitted a total of eight monthly reports (see Table 2). The main framework through which we were able to analyze the maternal representations was a graphical timeline of the violence and the bodily representation of the statutory groups that represent their family situation. The various representations and dramatizations give rise to the narrative of abandonment that was experienced at the hands of the executioner, who is also the life partner and father of the children; this narrative leads to the difficulty in seeing in their own mother the lever that activates the difficult process of emancipation.

In Italy, the psychodrama group was initially made up of eight people that completed a total of seven monthly reports (see Table 2). The activities that were initiated by the psychodramatists permitted to get to significant representations of the maternal, through the description of the social atoms, of the emotions and of activities about family roles. Even in this group, ambivalent aspects between the positive and the negative relationship emerges. In contrast to the other countries however, the focus was placed on the negative aspects including: devaluation and intrusiveness, aspects that evidence the difficulty in the relationship, whereby the mother tries to become part of her daughter's life, but in order to criticize her instead of trying to understand her difficulties and trying to help her in overcoming them.

Romania had two groups of psychodrama with a total of 15 participants and they also sent in monthly reports on their activities (see Table 2). They proposed various activities to develop the more complex aspects of the maternal and in particular the ambivalence between the need for affection and withholding it, pondering on the difference between the ideal mother and the "real" mother. From the reports, it emerges that the real mother is violent and the relationship with her is characterized by her desire to crystallize the roles, thus preventing any changes. All the women expressed a desire not to take on similar behaviours with their own children and wished to acquire additional skills to improve. This strong motivation arose from the conscious realization that they were involuntarily triggering relational mechanism similar to those of their mother and that they wanted to change this situation.

Conclusion

From the Atlas.ti encoding, some important maternal representations emerged across all six countries. For the victims, the mother is "the one that teaches" and the relationship with her is seen as a function of the acquisition of fundamental existential skills, all related to intimate relationships. In particular the mother has a profound influence on the creation of the maternal identity of the daughter, which results in disappointments about positive expectations with respect to this model, that now must be challenged in order to change the state of affairs. As described below, psychodrama enabled the emergence of three substantially negative points as well as the availability of a positive solution consisting precisely in change.

1. "My mother taught me violence:" this first part is linked to the figure of the mother that relegates women to the home and domestic sphere because the woman is required to take care of the needs of others. Intrusiveness and depreciation are the tools the mother uses to control and that prevent the daughter from breaking free from this traditional stereotype. The inability to leave this prison of submission is perceived as a form of violence. (see Graphic 1).

2. "My mother did not teach me anything": the mother is seen as incapable not only of managing intimate relationships, but also of paving the way for social accomplishments. The maternal is experienced as a "black hole" that takes away strength and goals, leaving behind an emotional residual of internal rage, which is inhibited and therefore becomes unmanageable even when it could be useful for self-protection. The mother is not only "absent" when the daughter who has been a victim of violence needs help, but also she is the one who has "taught her to be a victim" with the mandate "to be quiet at home." From this teaching and from the internalized imperative of making herself available to others and their needs and requests instead of listening to herself, comes the lack of awareness on the part of victims of their own needs and also of not been able to recognize their own resources (see Graphic 2).

3. "My mother is critical:" one of the factors that leads to the difficulty of overcoming the victim condition is the internal voice of the maternal critic, from where low selfesteem arises, stemming from feeling unable to effectively carry-out what has been taught. The mother that judges is very strong because it is to her that the daughter turns to find an answer to her needs, while the response received is a devaluating judgement of being a failure. (see Graphic 3).

4. "Mothering herself:" the three key points discussed above have been worked-on through the use of psychodrama in all the countries via the creation of opportunities for discussion with the possibility of having the participants "mother themselves" through a process that allows them to: a) distance themselves from the maternal vicious cycle of need/negative judgement/devaluation/blame; b) distance themselves from the pain arising from the lack of maternal support; c) experience a change in interpersonal skills learned in the family and move from a passive victim role to becoming master of their own destiny. (see Graphic 4).

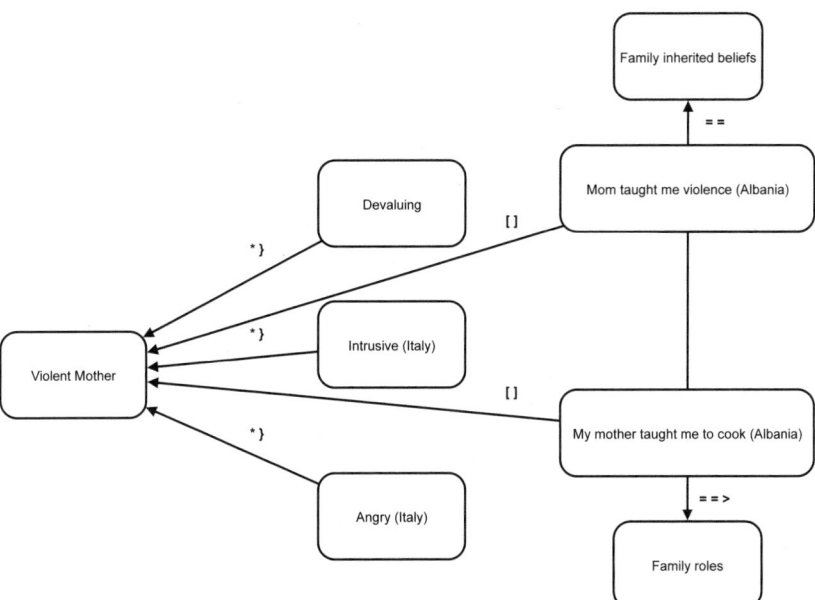

Graphic 1: Violence from mother

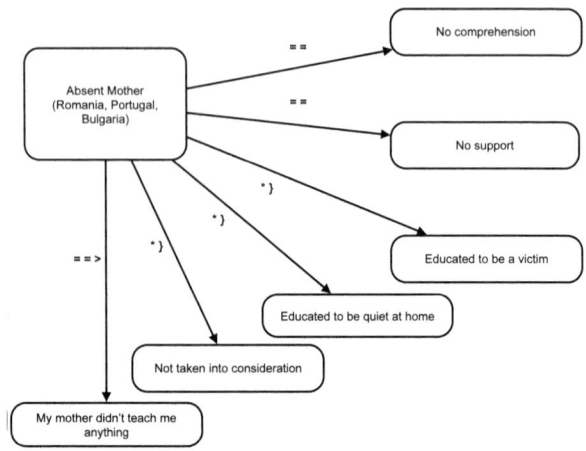

Graphic 2: Mother unable to teach

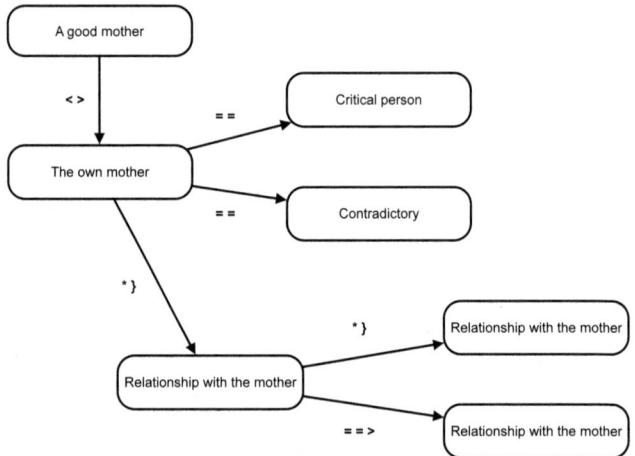

Graphic 3: Under maternal judgment

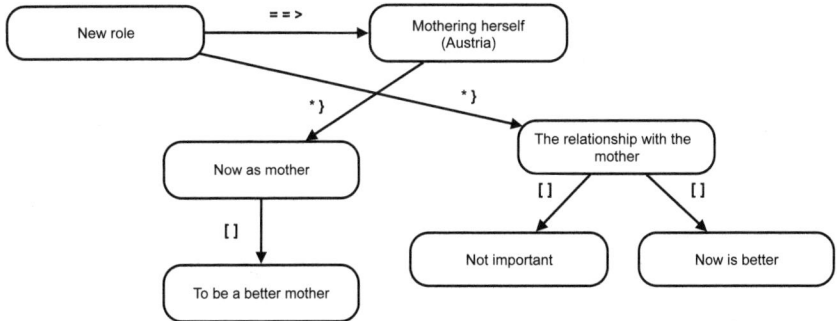

Graphic 4: Self-mothering

We can therefore conclude that the psychodrama sessions developed aspects relative to the maternal teaching relationship and the victim role which was taught. The deconstruction of this facet through psychodrama enabled the women to recognize the internalized maternal judge, that imposes compliance with the traditional feminine roles of subservience. Of particular relevance is the fact that despite the painful experience, the desire to be good mothers takes on a significant value that empowers women to believe in change. From this basic motivation comes the possibility for victims to recognize their own needs and fulfil them by becoming "mothers of themselves". To be a mother of yourself means to recognize your own limits, accepting them when they are insurmountable. From this realization comes the possibility to break free from the guilt and internalized devaluation that crystallizes the subordinate role taken on.

References

Adelman, M., Haldane H. & Wies, J. R. (2012). Mobilizing Culture as an Asset A Transdisciplinary Effort to Rethink Gender Violence. *Violence Against Women, 18*(6), 691–700.

Barker, D. & Feiner, S. F. (2004). *Liberating Economics: Feminist Perspectives on Families, Work, and Globalization.* Ann Arbor: University of Michigan Press.

Bateson, G. (1972). *Steps to an Ecology of Mind: Collected Essays in Anthropology, Psychiatry, Evolution, and Epistemology.* Chicago: University of Chicago Press.

Becker, G. S. & Becker, G. S. (1991). *A Treatise on the Family, Enlarged Edition.* London: Harvard University Press.

Beneria, L. (1979). Reproduction, production and the sexual division of labour. *Cambridge journal of economics, 3*(3): 203–225.

Blum, L. M. (2007). Mother-Blame in the Prozac Nation Raising Kids with Invisible Disabilities. *Gender & Society, 21*(2), 202–226.

Chodorow, N. (1978). *The Reproduction of Mothering, Psychoanalysis and the Sociology of Gender* (2nd ed., 1999). Berkeley: University of California Press.

Chodorow, N. (1989). *Feminism and Psychoanalytic Theory*. New Haven: Yale University Press.

Faludi, S. (1991). *Backlash: The undeclared war against American women*. New York: Doubleday.

Ferber, M. A. & Nelson, J. A. (2003). Beyond Economic Man, ten years later. In M. A. Ferber and J. A. Nelson (Eds.), *Feminist Economics Today: Beyond Economic Man* (pp. 1–32). Chicago: Chicago University Press.

Fitzpatrick, M. (2009). *Defeating autism: A damaging delusion*. Oxon UK: Routledge.

Hewitson, G. J. (2003). Domestic Labor and Gender Identity: Are All Women Carers? In D. K. Barker & J. Kuiper (Eds.), *Toward a Feminist Philosophy of Economics* (pp. 266–284). London: Routledge,.

Ladd-Taylor, M. & Umansky, L. (Eds.). (1998). *"Bad" Mothers: The Politics of Blame in Twentieth-Century America*. New York: New York University Press.

Laidler, K. J. & Mann, R. M. (2008). *Anti-feminist backlash and gender-relevant crime initiatives in the global context*. Feminist Criminology, 3, 79–81.

Lanci V., Sue, J. & Ryan, E. (1997). *Motherhood at the crossroads: Meeting the challenge of a changing role*. New York: Insight Books.

Lawler, S. (2000). *Mothering the Self*. London: Routledge.

Messing, J. T., Adelman, M. & Durfee, A. (2012). Gender violence and trans-disciplinarity. *Gender Violence, Violence Against Women, 18*(6), 641-52.

Moreno, J. L. (1953). *Who shall survive?: Foundations of sociometry, group psychotherapy and sociodrama* (Student edition by American Society of Group Psychotherapy & Psychodrama, 1993). Beacon N.Y.: Beacon House Inc.

Moreno, J. L. (1972). *Psychodrama First Volume Fourth edition*. Beacon N.Y.: Beacon House Inc.

Muhr, T. (1991). Atlas/ti – a prototype for the support of text interpretation. *Qualitative sociology, 14*(4), 349–371.

Persky, J. (1995). Retrospectives: The Ethology of Homo Economicus. *The Journal of Economic Perspectives, 9*(2), 221–231.

Ridgeway, C. L. (2001). Gender, Status, and Leadership. *Journal of Social Issues, 57*(4), 637–655.

Suttie Ian D. (1988). *The origins of love and hate*. London: Free Association Books.

Ven, T. V. & Vander Ven. M. (2003). Exploring Patterns of Mother-Blaming in Anorexia Scholarship: A Study in the Sociology of Knowledge. *Human Studies, 26*(1), 97–119.

Walker, M. U. (1998). *Moral Understandings*. New York: Routledge.

Zucchermaglio, C. (2002). *Psicologia culturale dei gruppi* [Psychology of groups]. Roma: Carocci.

"You made your bed, now you can lie in it": the biodynamic understanding of healing the social mechanisms keeping women in abusive relationships

Denise Saint Arnault, Mary Molloy, Sharon O'Halloran, Gill Bell

Social networks can both give support as well as create social constraints to help seeking, leaving abusive relationships, and enabling autonomy for women. These cultural mores and expectations are unspoken, ubiquitous, and "normal" for the person within her environment. While the person may consciously recognize them as a source of pain and constraint, they are often at a loss about to *how* to challenge them. Moreover, the community continues to operate by these fears and rules, making spontaneous free choice seem unattainable. In Biodynamic Psychology (BP), we understand that social and cultural rules can be transmitted across generations unconsciously, in the form of an energetic and emotional charge. The charge is carried within the cells and tissues of the individuals in the community. BP recognizes that individual cells can be bathed in these fears and constraints since before her birth, making the prospect of freeing from them seem impossible. This charge, held in the cells and tissues, can debilitate help seeking and keep generations of women in unhealthy situations. Therefore, BP theorizes that social change, as well as individual health, occurs at the cellular level. In this paper, we will link social change with this cellular change, and provide examples from our Biodynamic intervention, designed to facilitate healing from domestic and sexual abuse.

Sociocultural rules for propriety and women's help seeking

Some authors have speculated that communities, especially other women, may regulate women's propriety and role enactment, and thereby constrain their ability to break away from long-held rules that keep women "in their proper place" (Bestor, 1996; Saint Arnault, 1998; Saint Arnault & Roles, 2012; Ishii-Kuntz, 1993). Many cultures emphasize the value of harmony, especially in rural communities where the security of individual families may rely on the good feelings of the rest of the community in times of stress or need (Marit, 2006). The belief that "everybody knows everybody" and everyone cares about what is going on in the community can impart a feeling of security. At the same time, the power of this interdependency can be used as an informal social control, including scrutiny and expectations for conformity.

Community expectations of proper behavior and how to act and live within small communities can be conveyed to individuals through gossip, or the threat of gossip. For example, anthropological research has examined the concept of "peace and quiet" as a central cultural category in Norwegian culture (Gullestad, 1984). This cultural belief was used to legitimize regulation of women's behavior. Citizens within this community controlled tensions and conflicts using avoidance, gossip, shunning and ostracism. In her study, entitled *Kitchen-table society*, which was a study of young women in a Norwegian suburb, Gullestad argued that "women's talk when they are together may be analyzed as a moral discourse about what is right and wrong" (Gullestad, 1984, p. 220). Gossip is an interaction among people whereby the talk centers around an evaluation of a person's behavior and this evaluation can be construed as a moral discourse within a community or a social group (Haugen & Villa, (2006). These activities are ways that communities "pass on" and enforce rules of conduct. Social control mechanisms, therefore, not only transmits cultural rules for propriety, but also enforce prescribed behaviors.

In Asia, the concept of harmonious social relationship and smooth functioning within the group also involves edicts about appropriate gender role behavior and gender specific social control. Behaviors that may cause conflict are seen as indicating deviance, which can be heard in the admonishment "the tall tree catches the wind" (Bestor, 1996; Saint Arnault, 1995; Johnson, 1995; Smith, 1961). Traditional Japanese cultural norms for women include the cultural concept of *ryoosai kenbo* (roughly translated as "good wives and wise mothers"). Modern women are expected to enact these roles, and this enactment is enforced through scrutiny, gossip and the possibility of ostracism (Bernstein, 1991; Haga, 1990; Hsia, 1996; Iwao, 1993; Nagawa, Teti & Lamb, 1992; Saint Arnault, 2002). Wolf also writes about social sanctions of gossip and ostracism in a rural village in Taiwan (Wolf, 1992).

In the fictional tale *Valley of the Squinting Windows,* rural life in Ireland is described (MacNamara, 1919). The power of gossip, public perception and social control are described as a functional form of an inward-looking society. In this segment, a woman recognizes that her community level status is derived from their perception that she is the embodiment of the ideal woman and mother, and this affords her with moral authority.

> The pride of her motherhood struck a high and resounding note in the life of the valley. Furthermore, it gave her authority to assert herself as a woman of remarkable standing amongst the people. She devoted her prerogative to the advancement of the Catholic Church. She manifested herself as one intensely interested in its welfare (MacNamara, 1919, p. 2).

The dark side of this lovely picture is that she must maintain her impeccable behavior in public, and the private inner workings of her home remains behind closed doors. In addition, she and others will *look askance* at each other's behaviors to maintain or widen the gap between women. In all of these examples, we can see how the power of informal social control of women can lie in the hands of the community, and can be enacted by women. In this way, control of women's behavior can be carried out by women's mothers, sisters, and other women within the community. In some cases, when women want to describe distress or suffering, seek help for their distress, or act in some way outside of the agreed upon social rules of conduct, these behaviors can be perceived as threating or deviant, generating a social response to keep women "in line." Moreover, even the fear that one will be discovered to be somehow improper, and the fear of being associated with someone who is somehow deviant, can exert a powerful force controlling women. This set of social forces can occur when women are in a domestic abuse situation; her efforts to tell others and to seek help for her safety can evoke censorship, reproach and shunning rather that the help she expects and needs. Even the fear that she will receive such a response can silence women. Since these fears and behaviors are cultural and generational, they exert a powerful disabling force for women. We theorize that these cultural edicts for proper behavior among women have been handed down across generations of mothers and daughters. This paper examines a unique and important Biodynamic (BD) perspective about how this cultural transmission of mores and behavioral prescriptions can get "under the skin". We understand that these conditional expectations carry with them an energetic weight or "charge" that operates beyond the physicality of any individual, and persists across generations. Despite the transpersonal nature of this charge, it can have compelling influences within communities as well as within any given individual. The BD intervention approach addresses the release of this emotional charge, which can liberate women from these potent internal forces, empowering her to more successfully engage with the external ones.

Biodynamic theories of energetic charge

Emotional charge can be stored in the body, and is referred to in BP as armouring. Armouring keeps the psychic and physical energy static, and the body is held in a chronic, permanent startle reflex. This muscular contraction prevents tensions and emotions from being released. Armouring is understood to occur in layers, from superficial to deep. In addition to storing tension and emotional pain, armouring traps bodily fluids and restricts blood and lymph circulation that would normally remove biochemical deposits. The concentration of metabolic residues in the body, such as adrenaline and lactic acid, repeatedly engages the sympathetic nervous system, keeping the person in a chronic state of hypervigilence or shock and often leading to re-traumatisation. Spontaneous decisions for one's own health and safety may be, therefore, disabled both externally by cultural and social constraints, as well as internally by armouring.

BP also theorizes that armouring occurs in the cell as well as in the muscles. When a cell is armoured, nervous impulses (also understood as energy or the "action potential"[1] of the cell) becomes trapped. The potential to act is encapsulated in the cell. This trapped energy, as well as the chronic recirculation of the trapped energy, can lead to feelings of anxiety, agitation, hopelessness, resignation, and the feeling that it is impossible to complete an action, even though the potential is there. In BD theory, there must be sufficient force for the action potential, or the energetic charge, to move across the threshold of the semipermeable cellular membrane, and to complete the interrupted impulse. It is this potential that the BD therapist is working with, facilitating the building of the charge to the degree that it can break through the armouring. When the charge is sufficient, it can create an opening in the cell membrane and allow permeability, understood as the ability for the charge to go through the armoured membrane, and clear its trapped energy. Once this energy is liberated, normal biological mechanisms remove hormonal and biochemical residues, referred to as normalization. The biological or somatic indicator is called psycho-peristalsis, which is the gut's role in healing and self-regulation (Boyesen, 1980; Saint Arnault, Molloy and O'Halloran, 2012). The healthy cell can now function normally, permeable again, and able to absorb nourishment and new information.

---

1   Action potential is theorized in physiology as a short-term change in the electrical potential on the surface of a cell (e.g. a nerve cell or muscle cell) in response to stimulation. This change in the electrical potential allows impulses to travel across the cellular membrane. During this process, a fraction of the neural cell membrane opens to let the positively charged ions into the cell and eliminate the negatively charged ions. This transmission of nervous impulses across the cellular membrane is referred to in BD theory as the zone of firing.

Biodynamic Psychodrama and transgenerational charge

The details of the Biodynamic perspective of psychodrama are published elsewhere (Saint Arnault, Molloy and O'Halloran, 2012). One of the Biodynamic psychodrama techniques that can be used to address interpersonal transmission of charge at the family, community or cultural level is to engage the person with the "negative," the "good" and the "ideal." In this technique the therapist or the group members can provide voice to the unconscious and embodied messages the woman has received from her mother, sisters, and community. In doing so, the energy necessary to meet the generations-old cultural fear and rules for proper conduct is beneficially re-constructed and built to become sufficient to enable release. Through Bio-dynamic psychodrama, people are given the safety and the tools needed to complete emotional cycles held in their bodies and minds have has prevented them from living their lives fully and spontaneously.

With the BD approach, psychodrama facilitates the process of "getting the trapped energy out". Rather than "going into" a past traumatic event, the person is invited to access or re-experience the past within a safe environment, for the purpose of completion of the action that was needed at that time. The BD therapist helps this to happen by "holding" the space; being supportive and encouraging; being totally present, fully attentive, non-judgemental, and by not interrupting the participants progression through the process described above. The focus of the therapist is in the "here and now" about a situation that may have happened "there and then" (but is not happening now). The therapist recognizes that "there and then," it was not possible or safe to express something or to have a response or reaction, or to take an action (e.g. to walk away or leave, or to defend oneself or another). The zone of firing is the turning point where the emotion is expressed, and the excess emotional charge is discharged. This clearing is fundamental and time is always given for this process. If not, vital emotional energy will still be used in maintaining the repression, and is therefore not available or accessible in everyday life. Biochemical residues are carried via the fluids in the body, through the blood vessels and lymphatic channels, down to the kidneys and out of the system. The bodily evidence of this is psycho-peristalsis, which is the biomarker used by the therapist to confirm that the natural healing process (which had been interrupted) has been restored. The energy becomes free from these residues, available to the person's capacity, enabling autonomous functioning.

Biodynamic vignettes

The kitchen table. It is in the morning after breakfast as the 8 women and the therapy team are gathered around the kitchen table. We have just viewed a political speech wherein the speaker described all of the social forces, whether in the schools, churches or communities, that collude to support and tolerate violence in the home. As we sat quietly around the kitchen table, one woman said her home has never felt like a place of safety, and that indeed, even years after leaving her abuser, she still locks the door to her bedroom. She whispered her realization, "I could have died; I could have been killed". With compassion, the women and the staff wept and mourned for this extreme vulnerability; that *all* women in domestic abuse *fear* in their own homes. We held the consciousness that women all over the world are living in this danger. The lead author reminded the group about the generally unspoken but extremely powerful ways that mothers and sisters control each other to remain in these abusive relationships; shaming, shunning and gossiping about those who try to break free. We sat together quietly, reflecting on how moments where women who gather at the kitchen table can also foster a beautiful healing (as we were having now) or can be used to hold women in their (culturally determined) proper place. The often heard metaphor, delivered from mother to daughter, "You made your bed, now you can lie in it", was discussed by women as one such mechanism. We worked with the importance of the symbolism of the kitchen table representing the possibilities of how women could instead conspire to help each other, and reframe our social power for good and health and support and strength and safety. However, the deepest and most important realization that each woman had, is that they had been living in the fear, every day and night, for years, that they, or their children, *could have been killed.* This recognition led to the beginning of clearing effects of the perhaps the deepest fear of all – the "death fright".

The ideal mother. Shannon was in her early forties with a history of abuse at the hands of her mother as well as her husband. She described being confused and stymied by the power of the messages she received from her mother and siblings to remain in her abusive marriage. Referring to these potent messages as "stigma," she felt overwhelmed by their continuing power in her life even years after her separation with her husband. She described repeated encounters with her mother where she felt shamed and judged. The lead therapist worked with Shannon to mobilize this long trapped energy by recruiting the group to voice the messages sent by the "negative mother." Almost immediately, Shannon went from animated and angry to "frozen". She spoke very slowly and quietly giving an occasional rebuttal, but after a few minutes, she became more focused and forceful. Finally, with the help of the therapist and the group, she was able to mobilize enough energy to express a strong, clear and resounding rejection of the messages, and of the power of that (negative) mother within her. After this expression, the therapist and the group began to voice positive and life affirming supportive messages that would have been sent by the "ideal" mother, the messages she had never heard. Again, Shannon was silent and confused, perhaps a little embarrassed, and somewhat rejecting of these messages. Over a few minutes, though, her body relaxed, her eyes focused, and her movements became gentle and soft. The therapist invited her to lie on a prepared mattress on the floor on her left side in the BD "recovery" position, and she was covered with a blanket. The therapist placed the stethoscope on her abdomen to verify that her psycho-peristalsis had been established, indicating that the energetic clearing was therefore taking place. Shannon rested, normalized, and slept peacefully for around 40 minutes in the group. When she awoke, she was glowing and calm, with color in her cheeks and a steady voice.

The controlling sisters. Fiona was married for over 20 years to her abuser, and had attempted many times to recruit support from her sisters to leave. However, she said that not only did her sisters belittle her; they supported her husband's position. Indeed, even after their divorce, she felt her sisters cast aspersions about her among themselves and gossiped about her with other community members. She felt locked in a system where her behavior was scrutinized and her efforts toward independence thwarted. In order to build the charge, and with the consent of Fiona to work with this material, the therapist and the group took on the role of her "negative" sisters, "criticizing" her at every turn. Fiona's diffuse and disabling feelings of indignation became focused, and she moved from an anxious and fretting style of speech to a calm and unyielding statement of her truth, making a resolute proclamation that these women would cease to have power over her life. This expression was in itself liberating for Fiona and it was important to support this by the therapist and group positively confirming her new and clear energy. Fiona rested in the group after this process and felt refreshed and a renewed sense of resolve.

Conclusion

We believe that the work needed to dismantle the intergenerational and cultural processes of charge are both cellular and also intensely social. The BD position about how energetic charge can "get under the skin" is similar to the popular theoretical analysis referred to as the biology of belief (Lipton, 2010; Giovannoli, 2000), which asserts that cultural, social and spiritual beliefs and values, and the emotional power they contain, becomes a part of individual-level cellular structures, such that they constrain perception and choice. This analysis suggests that behavioral expectations and constraints are programmed into our physiology from birth. We agree that this belief system, indeed, gets into our biology, and uses the concepts of cellular discharge as a mechanism to promote individual and cultural change.

The work of BD psychodrama for domestic abuse, we believe, should be carried out in a group. This group can represent the power of women at the kitchen table – the power to witness and support health, and to use our social power to transform cultural edicts. Indeed, this group becomes a dynamic force to support the transmission of a new cultural norm that rejects constraint and silencing, has the power to understand context, society and interdependence, and that supports actualization and autonomy. We can become a source of a new culture that resists control, supports freedom and creates safety for all people.

All of the women who participated in our groups were functioning: they were working, raising their children, engaging with the courts, negotiating with their former abuser and seeking healing. However, the charge of generations of social and cultural fears, constraints and rules, as well as their individual experiences of domestic and sexual abuse, remained in their cells and tissues. While this charge constrained their full capacity, it also motivated them to seek deeper healing. However, only when this trapped energy is fully released from their bodies and minds can these women determine their true needs, thrive, and engage in an empowered way to resist the cultural and social forces that had operated to keep them "in their place."

References

Bernstein, G. L. (1991). *Recreating Japanese Women 1600-1945: Edited by Gail Lee Bernstein*. Oxford: University of California Press.

Bestor, T. C. (1996). Forging tradition: social life and identity in a Tokyo neighborhood. In G. Gmelch & W. P. Zenner (Eds.), *Urban Life: Readings in Urban Anthropology* (pp. 524–547). Prospenct Heights: Waveland Press.

Giovannoli, J. (2000). *The Biology of Belief: How Our Biology Biases Our Beliefs & Perceptions*. New York: Rosetta Press, Inc.

Gullestad, M. (1984). *Kitchen-table Society: a Case Study of the Family Life and Friendships of Young Working-class Mothers in Urban Norway*. Oslo: Universitetsforlaget.

Haga N. (1990). *Ryoosai Kenbo* (Good wife and wise Mothers). Tokyo: Yuzankaku.

Haugen, M. S. & Villa, M. (2006). Big Brother in rural societies: "Youths" discourses on gossip. *Norsk Geografisk Tidsskrift-Norwegian Journal of Geography, 60*(3), 209–216.

Hsia, H.C. & S., J. H. (1996). Rethinking the roles of the Japanese women. *Journal of Comparative Family Studies, 27*, 309.
Ishii-Kuntz, M. (1993). Japanese fathers: Work demands and family roles. In C.J. Hood (Eds.), *Men, work and family.* Newbury Park: Sage publication.
Iwao, S. (1993). *Japanese Woman.* Cambridge: Simon and Schuster.
Johnson, F. A. (1995). *Dependency and Japanese Socialization: Psychoanalytic and Anthropological Investigations Into Amae.* New York: NYU Press.
Lipton, B. H. (2010). *The Biology of Belief: Unleashing the Power of Consciousness, Matter and Miracles: Easyread Large Edition.* United States: ReadHowYouWant.com.
MacNamara, B. (1919). *The Valley of the Squinting Windows.* New York: Brentano's.
Nakagawa, M., Douglas, M. T. & Michael E. L. (1992). An ecological study of child-mother attachments among Japanese sojourners in the United States. *Developmental Psychology, 28*(4), 584–592.
Saint Arnault, D. M. & Roles D. J. (2012). Social networks and the maintenance of conformity: Japanese sojourner women. *International Journal of Culture and Mental Health, 5*(2), 77–93.
Saint Arnault, D. M. (2002). Help-Seeking and Social Support in Japanese Sojourners. *Western Journal of Nursing Research, 24*(3), 295–306.
Saint Arnault, D. M. (1998). *Japanese company wives living in America: Culture, social relationships and self* (PhD diss.). Wayne State University.
Smith, R. J. (1961). The Japanese Rural Community: Norms, Sanctions, and Ostracism1. *American Anthropologist, 63*(3), 522–533.
Wolf, M. (1992). *A Thrice-Told Tale: Feminism, Postmodernism, and Ethnographic Responsibility.* Stanford, California: Stanford University Press.

Transgenerational Echoes of Violence: Jungian Psychodrama as a Path to Individuation

Leandra Perrotta

Women with violent transgenerational history tend to reiterate dysfunctional patterns in their relationships (Faimberg, 2005), as unprocessed traumatic events find a way of manifesting themselves in subsequent generations and resurfacing in the present. This paper discusses the case of Irina and how Jungian Psychodrama helped her to work through her traumatic experience, exorcise her fear of mental illness, and free herself from a painful and unacceptable past.

The objective of Jungian Psychodrama (Gasseau & Perrotta, 2012) is therapeutic: starting from dreams and everyday reality, transgenerational themes are analysed to bring conscious and unconscious elements of the psyche into balance and relief and meaning to psychological suffering.

Thirty-year old Irina from Russia asked to join the psychodrama group because she had "problems regarding men" and because she suffered from numerous psychosomatic symptoms. She came from a dysfunctional family and had a story of unresolved pain relating to a former relationship with an abusive partner and the fear of reliving this experience[1].

Irina's dreams

Irina's personal narrative was imbued with transgenerational echoes (Perrotta, 2011) of violence and seemed to bear the influence of scripts inherited from previous generations. Irina grew up in a military area at the Russian border. Her mother was depressed, unloving and dependent upon an abusive father who sexualized his relationship with Irina as soon as she entered puberty.

---

1   Symbolically equivalent substitutions and other minor changes have been made in the presentation of this clinical case in order to protect the identity of the patient involved.

In order to exorcise her feelings of guilt and fear of mental illness, she fled to Europe. Scared of relationships with men, she felt lacking in relational intelligence and regarded emotional ties as places of enmeshment and dependency.

At first, Irina's persecutory ideas made it difficult for her to enact real-life situations. Fascinated by the oneiric world however, she introduced herself to the group by sharing many dreams, filled with military figures, dead people, collective violence and an incumbent, threatening extra-terrestrial eye.

Quite a few weeks went by before Irina was willing to enact her first dream on stage. Irina was in a hospital bed. A medical doctor was at the far end of the room, sitting on a chair and keeping her under observation. A nurse approached her, carrying an enormous needle, and injected her with a black liquid which paralysed her. In the soliloquy, she declared she couldn't feel any emotions but only a "cold death inside". She refused to enact a scene in association to her dream and confessed her fear that her dreams proved she was "transitioning into insanity".

Dreams are a privileged area of exploration for Jungian psychodramatists who work on individuation and transgenerational themes. Dreams provide access into unconscious areas of life and are an elective tool that facilitates the construction and awareness of a new and more authentic self-image in comparison to the partial one conveyed through the psychogenealogical code. Enacting dreams allows the therapist to complexify the patient's identity, enabling a process of disidentification from acritically interiorized operative models, and the integration of split-off contents of the psyche.

Irina's developing body caught her father's attention upon entering puberty. The abuse permeated the confines of her ego, deeply modifying her psychic economy. In order to survive, Irina's body became a "container of symptoms", incapable of expressing her pain in any other way.

As a teenager, she experienced her father's approaches with ambivalent emotions: fear but also gratification for being chosen as his object of love. Clinging to the possibility of a normal relationship, Irina found herself complying with her father's every desire but felt betrayed by her mother's silence and inability to protect her. The oscillation between violence and tenderness could not be harboured or assimilated by Irina in a unified inner image and the reciprocally incompatible relational models made her feel she was "going mad".

Silence is a fundamental process in the transgenerational dynamic (Tisseron, 1996). Unable to speak the unspeakable, the unbearable emotions caused by the conspiracy of silence in her family had obstructed Irina's process of individuation whereby her psyche could develop and gradually expand its consciousness.

Individuation (Jung & von Franz, 1964) describes the psychic process by which the individual Self develops out of an undifferentiated unconscious.

Irina's inability to individuate from the transgenerational prescriptions of her family had trapped her in a role of passivity.

In the first dream Irina enacted, she felt invaded and traumatized and unable to signify and give meaning to her story. Irina's mother had injected a needle of disturbing affects into her and the transgenerational prescription ordering her not to rebel against the "cold death inside" had paralysed the development of her symbolic capacity.

A few more weeks went by before Irina agreed to enacting another dream. Terrified and trembling, she found herself in a slaughter house filled with hundreds of live cows and sheep whose skin has been removed. They were standing in absolute silence but in obvious agony. Their eyes had been gouged out but the remaining holes were shining with a strange light.

Irina associated her dream to a painful event in her past and enacted a scene from her early adolescence when she was at the beach with her family. Her father inappropriately caressed her and she felt her eyes dim and her "skin starting to burn" when he touched her with his hands.

From that moment onwards, she had developed "blinding" headaches and a chronic form of dermatitis with symptoms including swelling, blisters and burn-like rashes which often appeared after her father touched her and which persisted all throughout her teenage years.

Irina shared with the group that she felt tortured by this "madness". She remembered wanting to run away when she was twelve but her mother had told her stories of unspeakable horror about the soldiers in the military camp near their home, and had warned her not to wander away because the "men would kidnap her". A week later, Irina dreamt of her childhood home. Her mother was on the threshold but her face was dark and wouldn't let her come inside.

Scared as she was to enact anything apart from her dreams, the director felt it was time for Irina to explore the inherited roles she unconsciously chose to play and encouraged her to build a transgenerational atom. The socio-metry of body postures and distance between auxiliary-egos would reveal the hidden structures and entanglements and function as affective regulators, expressing her psychogenealogical *gestalt* in the here and now.

Irina modelled the psychodramatic sculpture hesitantly, an enactment she knew would portray the dynamic pattern of shifting alliances, hidden beliefs and emotional currents through the use of metaphoric and analogical language. The mise en scène revealed the forbidden agendas and triangulations of her family and ancestors. Three persons in particular stood out in the proxemics: her grandmother Irina and her great-grandmother Natasha, who were placed hand in hand with Irina's alter ego. Slightly further away, Irina's father seemed to clamour for attention, trying to build a bridge of privileged communication with her.

Irina however, had forgotten to place her mother in the scene. The conspicuous omission was not pointed out straight away, as it was important for Irina to choose which relations were to be placed on stage. When the sculpture was complete however, and her mother's absence was suggested to her, Irina froze and buried her face in her hands. Irina's mother was significantly absent in her inner theatre of relations.

Her grandmother Irina – bearing her same name – was said to be insane. After role reversing with her, Irina had a powerful insight as to how her grandmother had been raped by the men at the military camp when she had wandered further away from the house than usual. Irina realized she was the first in her family to speak of this out loud and that her grandmother had been locked up in a psychiatric ward not because of insanity but because she had been a victim of violence.

Her great-grandmother Natasha had an alcoholic and violent husband and had borne twelve children of which three had died young. Natasha had been a free spirit and had always dreamt of travelling but her right leg had been amputated due to diabetes-related complications. Irina felt her strong legacy and expressed feelings of loyalty towards her. She recognized that she had fulfilled her great-grandmother's wish to travel but she had also amputated her own freedom by neglecting her inherent tendency to self-determination and her ability to "stand up on her own legs".

The term "invisible loyalty" (Boszormenyi-Nagy & Spark, 1973) is evocative because it explains the phenomenon that takes place in the family patchwork of unconscious expectations. Invisible loyalty is a systemic force that is functional to transgenerational homeostasis. Irina's great-grandmother did not live the life she wanted to and Irina acknowledged that she risked repeating her script.

Irina went on to enact a deeply emotional encounter with her great-grandmother. Natasha thanked her for her loyalty but encouraged her to live her own life. Her message to Irina was, "Think with your heart and learn to protect yourself".

Transgenerational psychodrama (Schützenberger, 2007) is a powerful means of shedding light on fantasmatic relations in the inner theatre of the mind. The re-enactment of transgenerational patterns, condensed into visual images, creates awareness which breaks cycles of repetition, deals with unfinished business and heals emotional wounds.

The following week, Irina dreamt that her mother was giving her electroshock treatment against her will and she woke up screaming. Irina's inner mother did not approve of her walking the path to individuation and planned on neutralizing her. Her mother's words to her in the dream were, "I will put an end to your suffering, even violently if necessary".

For several weeks after this drama, Irina was taciturn in the group, in the attempt to work through the deep meaning of the plays dramatized up until that moment. She shared that it was difficult for her to speak and that she only wanted to "sit and watch". Indeed, she sat silently in the circle of the group and let the other group members take care of her with tender and supportive words.

After a long period of silence, she exclaimed she had a dream to tell but that she didn't want to enact it. She dreamt there was a beautiful tree laden with flowers and fruit. A tractor approached and razed everything to the ground. Nothing living was left. The remains looked like bleeding, minced meat. An alien presence, in the shape of an eye, dripping human blood and organic material, hovered in the sky. Irina commented that she felt her mother was "spying on her".

The "phantom in the crypt" (Abraham & Török, 1978) is a concept which describes a formation in the dynamic unconscious caused by family secrets that are passed down through generations. The phantom is formed by the cryptic burial of unspeakable shame, an inaccessible sepulchre of secrets which was often expressed in Irina's dreams in the shape of a giant, extra-terrestrial eye observing her from the sky.

The phantom represents the energy of secrets buried in Irina's unconscious, energy transmitted from generation to generation with the characteristic of never emerging to consciousness. Past generations had chosen to cover up the abuse perpetrated upon women and the transgenerational mandate to the women in the family had prescribed them to "bear the unbearable".

Irina felt caught in a psychogenealogical trap. The secrets had broken through the confines of her psychic skin and had become a pain which lived on in the unconscious as a constellation of split-off energy. The phantom in the crypt was causing Irina to suffer.

Secrets in the family are pathogenetic because the very act of producing and perpetrating a secret actively expropriates psychic parts. It is not the secrets themselves but the concealment that produces pathology. Irina's initial declaration to the group of being "unable to speak" was the consequence of the contact between these two registers, an impossible and paradoxical dialectic.

In their compelling work, Schützenberger and Devroede (2003) write that a transgenerational illness of secrets is sometimes created in families when emotions and feelings are never expressed. They argue that children should consider forgoing their relationship and cutting ties with their patho-genetic parents if they want to preserve their emotional and psychic integrity.

The therapeutic aim was to help Irina identify the phantom in the crypt, cradle of toxic transgenerational secrets, so that she could reframe her traumatic story through the corrective experience of psychodrama, transform her psychic strife and become the origin and cause of her present.

As the months went by, Irina's trust built up and she shared more intimate and profound issues with the group. Irina started to question her fear of relationships with men and intuited that it had to do with the legacy inherited from the female members of her family who had given up personal emancipation and had annulled themselves in a position of strong dependency on men.

One day, Irina told the group that her ex-fiancé had obliged her to recite the mantra "I hate my body" while making her visualize her body as an inside-out sock. She played this scene and in the soliloquy admitted to feeling humiliated. She described the behaviour of her ex-partner as "terrifying" and "intent on breaking my will to live". She associated the cruel behaviour of her ex-fiancé to her father's abuse and to her old habit of "bearing the unbearable".

The following session, Irina asked if she could be a protagonist. The group was surprised by the assertiveness of this usually quiet and shy young woman, and encouraged her. Irina had started to realize that psychodrama was a privileged way of working through new meanings and creating a safe space for meta-cognitive and reflective thinking.

Irina enacted a scene in which her father stumbled through the door late at night, drunk and raging. Her father's slurring and seductively aggressive behaviour made Irina seek refuge in her mother's arms but her mother pushed her away and scolded her, telling her not to "exaggerate as usual". When Irina role reversed with her father, her facial expressions manifested dark anger whereas her mind was "blank as fog". In her mother's role, she felt crushed by the weight of denial and wrapped in a cloak of secrets. When asked to give a message to her mother, she cried out to her: "you didn't protect me, you are dead to me!"

Irina said she felt sadness invade her like a black octopus colonizing her bowels with its many tentacles. Repeated violence had caused Irina to identify with a "dead mother" complex (Green, 1983), a maternal object who drags her children into the underworld, producing feelings of impotence and psychic nonlife through the generations. As the guardian of unresolved transgenerational toxicity, Irina started to feel the urgent need to give voice to the unspeakable and stage a healing ritual of recognition of the phantom in the crypt.

Encouraged to name the tentacles of this black octopus, Irina accepted to go on stage and started to call out her own name in many different voices, ranging from a scolding and aggressive tone to a low, subdued and depressive voice to a silent surrendering whisper: the many voices she had heard from her childhood belonging to her mother.

The director encouraged Irina to play the mother she needed and desired. It was a simple image. Irina chose a very maternal woman from the group to play her mother and in her mother's role, she took Irina into her arms and read her a bedtime story. During the soliloquy, Irina sighed as she felt the image of a new mother growing within her and declared, "It is never too late to have a happy childhood".

A few sessions later, the director decided to explore the transgenerational instance of the dead mother by inviting Irina to create her matriline, a generational line of descent from her female ancestors all the way down to her symbolic daughter as the last descendant. This psychogenealogical drama provoked strong, emotional reactions of pain in Irina but allowed her to recognize the dimension of denial and passivity in her mother, the role of victim and the phantom of madness in her grandmother, and the aspect of hindered emancipation and sexual abuse legitimized by wedlock in her great-grandmother.

Next to the women, Irina placed an indistinct group of men, with uniformly aggressive features and threatening postures. These men "without a name" represented the inner violence of the male with which Irina had to reckon very early in her life. The women seemed to be unaware of the men and helplessly suffered from their tyranny.

The dead mother complex had triggered a profound state of impotence and passiveness along the generations, creating tragic consequences for the women. Irina realized she had to learn to use the therapeutic space of the stage to interrupt the cycle of transgenerational necrophilia and infuse new life into the maternal object.

Irina was starting to intuit the associations between apparently unconnected meanings. Two years later, Irina told the group about a dream she had in which there was a light in the sky but this time it was not a threatening, extraterrestrial eye but a patchwork of stars moving about in the shape of a mandala.

Irina played the dream and when invited to continue the dream as she wished, she climbed up to the highest mountain peak and lay down on a flat rock to contemplate the sky. The stars were shining and creating vortexes of light. Irina role reversed with one of the stars of the mandala and gave herself a message: "this is the archetype of all archetypes". It was still hard for Irina to contact her emotions because this had meant for too long to connect with the most painful parts of herself. However, Irina's nonverbal expressions conveyed a serenity which grazed her expression for the first time.

Irina took her own role again and the group echoed her message three times as in a sacred ritual. Touched, Irina finally wept. She acknowledged the path she needed to climb was still very steep but she was also aware that the mandala archetype, on the path to individuation, symbolized the goal and the destination, a place of creative possibility and self-realization.

Conclusion

Irina's dreams, played on the stage, conveyed deep messages from the unconscious and facilitated the creation of new *gestalts*. Jungian psychodrama aided her in softening the rigid confines of her inner roles, crystallized by transgenerational prescriptions and encouraged her to embark on an inner voyage of individuation towards new awareness and the exploration of new roles (Perrotta, 2009).

Jungian psychodrama is reparative. Transgenerational work helped Irina to refuse the pathological identification with her ancestors. She was able to shed light on her ghosts in the protective and containing space of the group and free herself from their persecutions.

The experience of emotional and cognitive reframing redefined the transpersonal matrix of Irina's family group and facilitated a dialectical discourse between identification and individuation from the transgenerational mandates that scripted female passivity, psychological paralysis and learned helplessness. Irina, like other disempowered women who had experienced individuation in psychodrama, could finally become an authentic protagonist of her life story.

References

Abraham, N., & Török, M. (1994). *The shell and the kernel: Renewals of psychoanalysis* (Vol. 1). Chicago: University Of Chicago Press

Boszormenyi-Nagy, I., & Spark, G. M. (1973). *Invisible loyalties: Reciprocity in intergenerational family therapy*. New York: Harper & Row

Faimberg, H. (2005). *The telescoping of generations: Listening to the narcissistic links between generations*. London: Routledge

Gasseau, M., & Perrotta, L. (2012). The Jungian approach: In situ supervision of psychodrama. In H. Krall, J. Fürst & P. Fontaine (Eds.), *Supervision in psychodrama: Experiential learning in psychotherapy and training* (pp. 37–56). Fachmedien Wiesbaden: Springer Verlag VS

Green, A. (1983). *Narcissisme de vie, narcissisme de mort* [Narcissism of life, death narcissism]. Paris: Les Editions de Minuit

Jung, C. G., & von Franz, M. L. (1964). *Man and his Symbols*. Garden City, N.Y.: Doubleday

Perrotta, L. (2009). Alchimia di sogni e rappresentazioni: L'osservazione nello psicodramma Junghiano [Alchemy of Dreams and Plays: Reflection in Jungian Psychodrama]. In M. Gasseau & R. Bernardini (Eds.), *Il sogno. dalla psicologia analitica allo psicodramma Junghiano* [Dreams. From

Anaytical Psychology to Jungian Psychodrama] (pp. 338–350). Milano: Franco Angeli

Perrotta, L. (2011). Introduction to the Italian edition of A. A. Schützenberger, *Psychogénéalogie: Guérir les blessures familiales et se retrouver soi* [Psychogenealogy: Healing Wounds and family back home]. Paris: Payot.

Schützenberger, A. A. (2007). *Psychogénéalogie. Guérir les blessures familiales et se retrouver soi* [Psychogenealogy. Heal wounds and family back home]. Paris: Payot.

Schützenberger, A. A., & Devroede, G. (2003). *Ces Enfants malades de leurs Parents* [These sick children from their parents]. Paris: Payot

Tisseron, S. (1996). *Secrets de famille: Mode d'emploi* [Family Secrets: Instructions]. Paris: Ramsay

From discourse to practice and back: the case of a project for victims of gender-based violence in Italy

Valentina Grosso Gonçalves, Elisabetta Camussi

Introduction

In the past several decades gender-based violence and family violence have elicited a great deal of attention from academics, clinicians and policy-makers. There is no longer any debate about the gravity of the issue or the devastating and far-reaching nature of its impact. This is a far cry from public attitudes and institutional responses to the problem no more than thirty to forty years ago, when gender violence was nowhere to be found on the political, research or social policy agenda of most Western countries (Nicolson, 2010). Today, with some delay compared to other European nations, gender violence begins to figure in the public agenda in Italy with relatively widespread (if still insufficient) shelter provision, services, intervention and prevention projects, media coverage, and campaigning (Manjoo, 2012). Evidence of such a change in public opinion on the subject includes a nation-wide, government funded campaign, promoted by the Ministry of Equal Opportunities, inviting women to denounce domestic violence and the relative institution of a dedicated, toll-free number for victims, on the one hand, and the ratification of a law defining and prohibiting stalking, on the other. Such a shift in attitudes and level of conscientiousness is undoubtedly the product of a steady wave of militant action and campaigning, advocacy, grassroots activism and research interest at both the national and the international level, all of which have contributed to shed some light on and draw attention to a phenomena that is so easily ignored, minimised, denied or distorted (Jecker, 1993; Zink, Jacobson, Saundra & Pabst, 2004; Romito, 2005). This combined effort – the majority of which stems from the vast body of feminist thought, practice and tradition deriving from the (national and international) women's movement of the 1970s – has had a direct and long-lasting effect on shaping legislation (Frattaroli & Teret,, 2006), health and social care practice (Humphreys, 2007), and public policy (Breckenridge & Mulroney, 2007). It

has also had a significant impact on attitudes, stereotypes and social representations of family violence and the role of women therein (Carlson &
Worden, 2005).

Feminist approaches, in particular, have played a major role in re-
defining and re-constructing the physical and mental abuse suffered by
women and children within the family from a 'normal', private and episodic
issue to a serious social problem, that implies criminal behaviour and
involves a power differential that can be understood as part of a specific
(patriarchal) cultural discourse. This has been important both in obtaining
visibility for and modifying general attitudes to the phenomenon, but also in
addressing how certain social representations and discourses of domestic
violence operate to sustain the dominant ideology and marginalize the voices
of victims through strategies of blaming, shaming and denial (Radford, 2003).
Pro-feminist critiques, moreover, have contributed to broadening the notion
of domestic violence or abuse to include non-physical forms of violence such
as psychological violence, intimidation, degradation, verbal abuse, humiliation,
economic deprivation, control and stalking under the umbrella term of
gender-based violence (United Nations, 1995).

The importance of the contribution of feminist approaches and of the
women's movement in both shifting attitudes, garnering public attention and
generating a wealth of services and service provision for victims of gender
violence cannot, and must not, be underestimated or minimised. As a theory
that builds upon the notion of patriarchy and patriarchal power as a system of
domination, however, most liberal feminist approaches bear similarities with
other sociological theories that emphasise the oppressive character of social
structures over individuals (Durkheim, 1982; Parsons, 1951; Bourdieu,
1977), as opposed to the social actors' ability to overcome oppression and/or
modify those same social structures.

Also, as various scholars in the field working from a psychological
paradigm have suggested, feminist analyses have deliberately chosen to
eschew both the issue of how couple dynamics and inter-individual factors
impact upon the generation, perpetuation and maintenance of the cycle of
violence and the question of why women often choose to stay with violent
partners and do not put an end to the processes of re-victimisation (Nicolson,
2010). Clinical and psychological approaches which have sought to address
these questions, on the other hand, have often neglected to consider how
individual differences and interpersonal dynamics occur within a set of
culturally-specific and situated social norms, and how personal subjectivity
and individual trajectories are inextricably inscribed in the social domain,
with the risk of minimising structural aspects of gender violence and
perpetuating some of the biases associated with an individualistic approach.

We propose a third perspective, which draws upon cultural and
discursive psychological theorisations of the relationship between cultural

discourses, social representations, and subjective positions, to investigate some of the challenges in developing truly empowering interventions for victims of gender-based family violence. Briefly stated, such a perspective builds upon the idea that individuals are at one and the same time the products of constraining social structures and discursive practices and ir-reducible, in their singularity, to socio-cultural determinants (Valsiner, 2000; Frosh, Phoenix & Pattman, 2003; Valsiner & Rosa, 2007). To the extent that subjects are necessarily inscribed in discourse and representations, which determine specific positions that a subject can come to occupy, such an inscription always leaves behind it a residual space, which becomes a space for subjective resistance, movement and re-signification (Butler, 1993).

The present paper draws upon the ethnographic data collected in a 3-year active participation in a local interagency project and shelter to support victims of gender-based violence to explore how a certain construction and re-presentation of gender-based violence, based on a liberal feminist paradigm, enables specific practices and degrees of agency and empowerment, both for the project's staff and for its participants, while curtailing other, possible actions. In order to do this we borrow from a broad social constructionist perspective (as outlined above) that assumes that social reality is the product of a co-constructed set of representations that are constantly negotiated by and between social actors. Case notes and interview extracts are used to explore how specific discourses and representations both inform and determine specific practices and strategies of intervention and their effects in determining individual women's space for agency and change.

Methodology

The field notes and case studies presented were collected during a three-year ethnographic study of a local, community-based interagency project for women escaping gender-based violence based in Torino, Italy, which we will call "the Shelter."

The Shelter

The Shelter offers survivors of gender violence who need temporary refuge the opportunity to stay in a protected space for a maximum of six months. The aim of the project, apart from further extending the network of available shelters for victims of gender violence, is to offer direct access to a safe refuge to women arriving directly from A&E departments.

Developed and promoted by a local association of volunteers historically connected with the women's movement (here called 'WAC'), who seek to offer help, guidance, support and representation to victims of gender-based violence, the project brings together a set of partners, including WAC: the funding agency of the project ('CP'), four Accident and Emergency (A&E) Departments, based in some of the city's largest hospitals; a non-profit organization that offers support to adults in need ('UP'); and another non-profit organization ('BC'), which provides the actual property that hosts the refuge.

The Shelter houses up to 8 women who can gain access either directly, via referral from A&E, or indirectly, via a first contact with WAC and subsequent referral to A&E. Upon arrival each woman is met and welcomed by one or more shelter worker, who explains how the project works, presents the refuge's set of rules and regulations and introduces her to the other guests. The women have a seven-day 'trial' period to decide if they wish to remain in the Shelter and continue with the project or leave, either to return home or to be redirected elsewhere. Should they decide to stay they discuss their situation with the shelter workers and agree to define a set of workable short, medium and long objectives they will attempt to pursue during their stay.[1] During the project all guests are supported by the project staff in finding alternative housing and employment (or in pursuing specific educational or training projects), where necessary, and have access to free legal support.[2]

Method and data analysis

Access to the field[3] was granted by the project's funding body, CP (a private foundation), in exchange for dedicated, periodic research reports evaluating the project's progress and abidance by good practice standards. This role involved taking part in and observing the weekly coordination meetings

---

1   Objectives will vary in relation to individual circumstances but generally include the following areas: health/medical, legal, housing, work, psychological.

2   The project staff is made up of: a project coordinator, a psychologist from WAC who is responsible for coordinating and managing the project team, two 'internal' shelter workers from BC, who maintain the day-to-day contact with the shelter's guests, supervise women's individual projects and oversee the smooth running of the refuge, an 'external' shelter worker from WAC who manages all of the Shelter's external contacts (from Social Services to hospitals and psychological services) and offers support in job-seeking and house-seeking and a general orientation as to the available resources in the area, as well as referring the women to the free legal support team, where necessary, and a researcher (the first author) responsible for monitoring the effective realisation of the project and producing.

3   Our role as researchers investigating interventions for victims of gender violence was always made explicit both to members of staff and to the Shelter's guests.

between the shelter workers and the coordinator, bi-annual plenary meetings with representatives from all of the projects' partners, and observing and sometimes actively participating in the activities conducted by the shelter workers both inside the refuge and in *liason* with other agencies, both statutory and voluntary. This role as a researcher with a double mandate – to report back to the project's funding body on the project's progress and to report to the scientific community on the viability of such a model in terms of interventions for victims of gender violence – proved very important in building trust with both the Shelter's staff and its residents.

A set of individual interviews were conducted both with the members of staff (who also took part in a set of focus groups at the onset of the project) and with the residents of the Shelter. The shelter residents who agreed to take part in the research (the vast majority), where possible, were interviewed at three different times: upon arrival (at weeks 2 or 3), halfway into their expected stay (at month 2 or 3), and shortly before departure. The interviews were semi-structured but largely "interviewee-centred" with the interviewer taking on a facilitative role and picking up on issues raised by the interviewee and encouraging them to develop and expand upon these.

The interviews were conducted using a narrative interviewing style to explore how the residents had arrived at the Shelter, what were their hopes, fears and expectations, their relationships with the other residents and with the various members of staff, as well as their history of violence (always to the extent and in the amount of detail that each woman wished to discuss it). The second interview aimed to explore changes in terms of expectations of the project, relationships with housemates and the project staff, perceptions of life in the Shelter, etc., as well as contradictions and gaps in material from the first interview. The third interview sought to offer the interviewees a chance to take an active part in the process of continuous improvement of the project by reflecting back and commenting upon their experience at the Shelter.

The data presented are based both on the observational material recorded in the field notes and on the textual material provided by the interviews. The analytic strategy used was to integrate a more general thematic analysis of the material, both observational and interview-based, with a more focused narrative analysis comparing a set of accounts presented by the residents themselves in the interviews with the accounts of those same residents given by the different project staff.

Results
The risks of a materialist approach: the cases of Fatima and Linda

One of the main tenets of the feminist approach is that patriarchal systems of power, by creating an unequal power relationship between men and women in favour of the former, make women vulnerable to violence and abuse. One of the main assumptions underlying such a stance is that many women do not leave abusive relationships or conditions largely because of the limited material resources available to them. Interventions therefore aim to increase financial and human resources available to women in order to support them in creating the conditions that will make them (economically and legally) independent from the abuser. This translates in a priority accorded to measures aimed at assisting those women who arrive at the refuge without an occupation to find a job. In the case of the Shelter, for example, this is done by helping residents compile or update their CV, putting them in contact with temping and recruitment agencies, or applying for a "paid work experience" with one the partner agency UP.[4]

With rising rates of unemployment in Italy, the Shelter has often resorted to "paid work experiences" to enable women who were new to the job market a chance to begin building their CV and earning an income. Fatima, one of the first women to arrive at the Shelter, was soon identified as an ideal candidate for such a post: at 19, she had just completed her secondary school studies and decided to leave her family home after years of physical violence and controlling behaviour on the part of her father, which had often, especially in the latter period, led Fatima to require hospitalization in A&E. When she arrives at the Shelter Fatima presents a series of physical ailments, connected with her history of abuse: she has frequent headaches, often coupled with blurred vision, difficulty sleeping, and throbbing pains in her legs and arms, where she hit the floor on one occasion when her father had thrown her down the stairs. She is referred to one of the project's partner hospitals for some medical tests, all of which indicate that Fatima's symptoms are not organic in origin, but appear to be psychosomatic consequences of her history of violence.

Fatima would like to continue with her studies and go to University but she has no form of income and, not being an Italian citizen, she does not qualify for any form of financial support to continue studying. The Shelter workers try to invite Fatima to reconsider her objectives, explaining that, if she wants to continue studying, she is going to have to support herself independently after leaving the project. They thus suggest Fatima apply for a

---

4   "Paid work experiences" [*borse lavoro*] are a relatively widespread tool used in Italy to support entry into the job market for young people or those who have little or no work experience and involve short term work placements (generally lasting three to six months) paid for by a third agency (i.e., not the employer).

"paid work experience" post, which would be sponsored one of the project partners. During one of the research interviews, Fatima confesses to being quite confused as to her future but has come to realise that the priority is achieving economic independence so as to not have to rely on her father for support. She therefore accepts the opportunity to undertake a "paid work experience" as a kitchen assistant in a hospital cafeteria. After a couple of weeks on the job Fatima's symptoms begin getting worse and she develops an acute pain in her right knee, which makes it difficult for her to walk or climb stairs and, in general, to be able to work. Instead of improving, her condition gets worse, with her knee swelling to the point that she is unable to bend her leg and is confined to the refuge. The medical tests performed seem to suggest that the problem does not have a physical cause but rather appears stress-related.

Due to her knee "injury" Fatima remains home on sick leave until her employer contacts the Shelter to suggest that, given her physical condition, she interrupt the work experience. The Shelter workers are worried about Fatima's future, once she leaves the refuge, due to "her difficulty in looking after herself properly and in maintaining a job" (SW1, staff coordination meeting4) and make Fatima aware of this, asking her to think again about how she plans to reach her objectives.

As the end of her available time at the Shelter grows near Fatima is contacted by her uncle, her father's brother, asking her to return home or, alternatively, to come and live with him and his family for a while. With no viable prospects on her road to independence and with nowhere else to go after leaving the refuge, Fatima decides to accept her uncle's offer to come and live with them for a while. Soon thereafter she decided to return home.

Like Fatima, when she arrives at the Shelter Linda is only 19 years old. Originally from Eastern Europe, she came to Italy one year ago looking for work. Soon after her arrival in B. she meets a fellow countryman, Dimitri and, a few months later, moves in with him and his mother. Not long after they move in together Dimitri becomes violent and aggressive and forces Linda to give him the whole of her wages as a private care worker. When he suggests they move to Switzerland where she would work as a highly paid escort under his management she decides to run away from B. and seek help in a larger city.

When Linda arrives at the Shelter, although her physical conditions are problematic (she suffers from severe back pain as a result of numerous car accidents, over and beyond the effects of the violence she was subjected to by her ex-boyfriend, and before that from her uncle) in she is keen to find a new job and begin a new life in Turin. It is agreed that Linda would be supported in an application for a "paid work experience" as a chambermaid in a hotel.

Once she begins working at the hotel, Linda's physical symptoms worsen and she often has to take sick days to recover. When, on one occasion, she forgets to call in sick, the hotel decides to terminate her contract and asks her not to return to work. Linda is disappointed and both she and the Shelter workers are worried about how she will be able to find and maintain a new house if she is not working.

During her time at the Shelter Linda also begins a new relationship with an older Italian man, Paolo. Although Linda expresses numerous doubts and uncertainties about this relationship, Paolo appears to be very keen on her and soon insists that Linda move in with him. In one interview she says, "I don't know if I'm in love with him...I don't know...probably not. But he's there, he's nice and all. And you know...maybe things could be easier if I just went to live with him instead of trying to make it on my own" (Linda, int3). Four months into her stay at the Shelter Linda decides to leave the project and move in with Paolo, who has agreed to support her financially so that she doesn't have to work.

For many of the women who arrive at the Shelter, one of the first requests made to the project staff is support in finding a job which will render them (at least financially) independent. At the same time, the number of successful insertions into the job market or "paid work experience" posts activated becomes an objective, quantifiable criteria used by funding agencies and monitoring committees to evaluate the "success" of a given project for victims of gender violence, somehow placing a certain pressure on organizations like the Shelter to respond to the resident's demand for employment with job opportunities or paid work experiences.

As the cases of Fatima and Linda illustrate, however, the reality of many cases of battered women who enter a refuge is more complex than the simple equation *improvement in material conditions = independence, autonomy and empowerment*, fostered by a certain version of the feminist discourse, would imply. For both Linda and Fatima, this is because, despite what both women seemed to demand on a conscious level – the opportunity to begin a new life away from a violent context – at a deeper and more unconscious level there appeared to be a different demand, as the intensification of their physical symptoms and the outcome of their individual projects at the Shelter seems to suggest. Given their particular histories of violence and the evident traumatic effects that such victimization produced, we might speculate that such a demand had more to do with a need to be assisted and taken care of than a specific need for emancipation. This does not mean, of course, that inter-ventions for victims of gender violence should concede and cater to such a demand, which might perhaps even be effective in the short term but would inevitably create a dependant relationship with the project staff and be ultimately disempowering for the women in the long term. But, as the cases of Fatima and Linda seem to suggest, what it does mean is that if such a demand (and subjective position) is not recognized and "worked through" with the women involved it will not simply disappear but rather will, on the one hand, hijack any intervention's (legitimate) attempts to help women gain greater independence via employment, for example, and, on the other hand, mean that such a demand will simply be redirected elsewhere.

Too much to handle: the case of Antonia

The final example we would like to present is the case of Antonia, a 35 year old Italian woman. She is referred to the project by her psychotherapist, Dr. G., who began exploring opportunities for alternative housing arrangements soon after Antonia began therapy, a couple of months earlier, once the details of her story became clear. Antonia has been a victim of multiple sexual abuse since she was a small child. Her first abuser was her godfather who first molested her at home, while her parents were away, and subsequently, when Antonia became a teenager, initiated her to a Satanic cult where she was the victim of ritualistic sexual abuse by both male and female members. Antonia claims that, during this period, she was also sexually abused by her older brother but that the incest stopped after a couple of years as her brother got a girlfriend and "lost interest" (Antonia, int1). The sexual and psychological violence perpetrated by cult members however, continued until the age of 30, even after she had left home and moved to another city.

At the age of 17, after a failed suicide attempt, she is referred to the school psychologist by one of her teachers, worried about the evident signs of depression and behavioural problems she is manifesting. Antonia trusts the psychologist and reveals that she is a victim of multiple sexual abuse, both within and outside the family. Given the gravity of the accusations, the psychologist chooses to breach patient confidentiality and gets in contact with Antonia's mother. When confronted with her daughter's story Antonia's mother denies the possibility that any abuse has taken place and suggests Antonia's problem is that she has "a much too vivid imagination" (Antonia, int1).

Following this episode, Antonia leaves high school and eventually manages to seek help by getting in contact with an organization that helps adults who have suffered sexual violence. Through contacts developed within this organization Antonia manages to leave her home and move first to M. (the city where the organization is based) and subsequently to R. (a larger city, further away), where she finds a job as a career. Her godfather, however, soon manages to track her down and threatens to harm her young nieces if she doesn't agree to take part in the cult's sexual practices on a regular basis, to which Antonia, terrified of what could happen if she didn't comply, reluctantly agrees. "When he called I had to get on the first train back home, which eventually meant I lost my job in R. as it was difficult to explain the reason behind all of those absences" (Antonia, int1).

The loss of her job in R. is a turning point in Antonia's life: she tells her godfather she has had enough of being blackmailed and threatens to go to the police and press charges if he doesn't stop harassing her. Her intimidation is taken seriously and both the psychological and sexual abuse comes to a halt but, now jobless and in a city where she has nowhere to stay, Antonia decides to return to her family home where she has been living with her parents for the past five years. During this period she has tried to "forget, forget it all" and "put the past behind [her]" (Antonia, int1), going back to school and working part time as a basketball coach.

The effects of her longstanding history of sexual and emotional abuse, however, were not erased as easily and Antonia has continued to suffer from vivid flashbacks, insomnia, difficulties sleeping, intrusive images and pseudo-hallucinations, dissociative behaviours and other symptoms of Post-Traumatic Stress Disorder (PTSD) which have led her to seek help first from her local Community Mental Health team, where she did not find the support she sought, and later from her current therapist, a female psychologist and psycho-therapist working for an nonprofit organization that offers specialist support for victims of childhood sexual violence.

Since her arrival in the Shelter, Antonia proved to be a particularly difficult resident for the Shelter workers: she was particularly demanding, often asking to for individual attention only to then refuse meetings when they are requested by staff, or giving Shelter workers detailed and explicit information about the abuse she was subjected to in ways they deemed "inappropriate and out of place" (SW2, weekly coordination meeting41). Antonia was also critical of some of the Shelter worker's interventions and refused to comply with some of their "project proposals". In particular, in the weekly co-ordination meeting the Shelter's staff team decided that it was too risky for Antonia to maintain regular contacts with her niece (her brother's daughter, who also lives next door to Antonia's parent's house) as this represented "an unsevered tie with the violent context she was escaping from" (Coordinator, weekly coordination meeting43) and informed her that if she continued meeting with her she would be "disregarding project regulations" (that posit no contacts with offenders) (SW2, weekly coordination meeting43).

The particular nature of Antonia's symptoms, coupled with the horrific details of her abuse which she had chosen to share with the Shelter workers (and not with the interviewer) provoked a great degree of anxiety in the Shelter's staff which manifested itself in doubts as to the authenticity of Antonia's story and lead to the decision to invite Antonia to make contact with her local Mental Health Team and undertake a psychiatric evaluation.

Antonia was appalled by this request, stating: "they want me to see a psychiatrist but I don't think I need a psychiatrist. I've been to a Mental Health Centre before and they assigned me to a male psychiatrist but I can't open up if it's a male doctor, I get anxious and scared. I don't want to see a psychiatrist unless it's someone my psychologist refers me to, someone I can trust. Plus I don't want to take drugs. I've taken prescription medication before and I felt horrible when I was on it. I wasn't myself any longer, I hated it. And that's all a psychiatrist does, prescribe medication, so why should I go? I have a therapist that I talk to, that I can work on these issues with, why do I need a psychiatrist? I'm not crazy!" (Antonia, int1). Likewise, her reaction to the possibility of severing all ties to the only member of her family she still had contacts with was of disbelief: "[my niece] is all I have left from my family... apart from my dogs, that obviously I can't see given that they live at my parents', she's all I've got in the way of family. Why should I stop seeing her? What has she done wrong? Nothing! She's an innocent victim of that family, like me. What have I done wrong to deserve this treatment? I feel like here I'm being forced to do things just like I've been forced by my brother and stepfather to do things before. I don't under-stand what the logic is" (Antonia, int2).

Antonia refuses to comply with either of the Shelter workers' requests and as a result is asked to make a decision as to whether she is seriously intending to pursue her project at the Shelter or not. Eventually she decides to leave the Shelter and return to her family home

Antonia was not the Shelter's first guest who had been a victim of sexual violence but she was the first and, to date, the only woman who had been subjected to sexual abuse as a child, to satanic ritual abuse, and to incest. The disturbing nature of her history of violence, which she chose to recount without censorship, seems to have provoked a sense of loss of control and of anxiety among the Shelter's staff which was dealt with defensively, by attempting to rigidly and authoritatively define Antonia's project and objectives during her stay at the Shelter. The effect on Antonia, from what emerged in the interviews, was to reduce her trust in the Shelter workers, to begin questioning her original decision to leave home, and to perceive a number of limitations on her possibilities of agency and change. Ultimately, Antonia's decision to return home seems to indicate that, whatever we think of her subjective position at the time of interview, the Shelter staff's interventions were not empowering for her, nor did they open the door to new possibilities.

It can be argued that Antonia's is a particular and extreme case, but we have chosen this example because it illustrates how a certain discourse on gender violence that both tends to eschew psychological interpretations and to believe there is a universally "right" and a "wrong" way to begin a path of emancipation from violence can easily slip into its own version of authoritarianism.

Conclusions

The question of how to develop successful interventions for victims of gender-based family violence is a pressing concern for both practice, policy and researchers. In this article we have sought to utilize case study data from an ethnographic study of a local, inter-agency project in Italy to explore how discourses and representations, with particular reference to liberal feminism, shape strategies and practices of intervention producing effects in terms of women's agency and empowerment. Our intention is not to criticize liberal feminism or accounts of gender violence that put the accent on the universal nature of patriarchy *per se* – on the contrary, we believe a feminist-inspired understanding of gender violence to be paramount in accounting for the phenomenon and in shaping interventions. Rather, by drawing upon the case of the Shelter and the examples cites, we hoped to show how a specific discourse, based on a liberal feminist paradigm, risks generating practices (and subjects) that produce quite the opposite of what it has set out to do: empower victims of gender violence to exercise agency and leave violent contexts.

On the one hand, this appears to happen when the psychological dimension of violence is disregarded in favour of an emphasis on material conditions and constraints, such as in the cases of Laura and Fatima. The failure to recognize and engage with the conscious and unconscious effects of trauma that violence tends to produce – both mental and physical – and focusing instead on material aspects – employment, housing, legal support – risks untimely interventions that, even if requested and apparently appreciated by women on a conscious level, cannot be sustained at a more unconscious level, producing disengagement. On the other hand, practices become disempowering for women when they are based on a version of feminism that privileges the universal of what "*should* be done" as opposed to the particular of "what *can* be done", that puts the focus on staff's "acquired knowledge" as opposed to remitting itself to the knowledge that each woman brings to bear on her life story, that loses sight of each individual woman's particular needs and desires and tries to reduce them to generic and preconceived notions of "right" or "wrong," of "adequate" or "inadequate" as Antonia's case shows.

How then to integrate these findings into shaping strategies for best practice and constructing future interventions for victims of gender violence? The feminist discourse began as a critique of the patriarchal order and its impositions on women, but when it is called upon to define practices and interventions it is no longer in a disadvantaged or minority position, but rather takes on the position of the *maître*, of the established order. What our findings seem to suggest is that if this position is not "faulty" or incomplete to some degree, if it does not truly and carefully listen to women's voices, expecting to work *for* as opposed to *with* victims and survivors, it risks reproducing the same authoritarian and disempowering logic as that of the patriarchal order.

References

Bourdieu, P. (1977). *Outline of a theory of practice*. Cambridge: Cambridge University Press.

Breckenridge, J. & Mulroney, J. (2007). Leaving violent relationships and avoiding homelessness – providing a choice for women and their children. *New South Wales Public Health Bulletin, 18*(6), 90–93.

Butler, J. (1993). *Bodies that matter: on the discursive limits of sex*. New York: Routledge.

Carlson, B. E. & Worden, A. P. (2005). Attitudes and Beliefs About Domestic Violence: Results of a Public Opinion Survey I. Definitions of Domestic Violence, Criminal Domestic Violence, and Prevalence. *Journal of Interpersonal Violence, 20*(10), 1197–1218.

Durkheim, E. (1982). *The rules of sociological method and selected texts on sociology and its methods*. New York: Free Press.

Frattaroli, S. & Teret, S. P. (2006). Understanding and Informing Policy Implementation A Case Study of the Domestic Violence Provisions of the Maryland Gun Violence Act. *Evaluation Review, 30*(3), 347–360.

Frosh, S., Phoenix, A. & Pattman, R. (2003). Taking a Stand: Using Psychoanalysis to Explore the Positioning of Subjects in Discourse. *British Journal of Social Psychology, 42*(1), 39–53.

Holloway, W. & Jefferson T. (2000). *Doing qualitative research differently*. London: Sage.

Humphreys, C. (2007). A Health Inequalities Perspective on Violence Against Women. *Health & Social Care in the Community, 15*(2), 120–127.

Jecker, N. S. (1993). Privacy beliefs and the violent family: Extending the ethical argument for physician intervention. *The Journal of the American Medical Association, 269*(6), 776–780.

Nicolson, P. (2010). *Domestic violence and psychology. A critical perspective*. London: Psychology Press.

Parsons, T. (1951). *The social system*. New York: Free Press.

Radford, J. (2003). Professionalising responses to domestic violence in the UK: definitional difficulties. *Safer Communities, 2*(1), 32–39.

Romito, P. (2005). *Un silenzio assordante: la violenza occultata su donne e minori* [A deafening silence: hidden violence on women and children]. Milano: Franco Angeli.

United Nations. *Beijing Declaration and Platform of Action, adopted at the Fourth World Conference on Women*, October 27, 1995. Retrieved from: http://www.unhcr.org/refworld/docid/3dde04324.html.

Valsiner, J. 2000. *Culture and human development.* London/Thousand Oaks, CA: Sage.

Valsiner, J. & Rosa, A. (2007). *The Cambridge Handbook of Socio-cultural Psychology.* Cambridge: Cambridge University Press.

Zink, T. C., Jacobson, J., Saundra, R. & Pabst, S. (2004). Hidden Victims: The Healthcare Needs and Experiences of Older Women in Abusive Relationships. *Journal of Women's Health, 13*(8), 898–908.

Part 3. Strategies and tools

Thinking, feeling, and acting: the use of the TAT test in short-term psychological consultations with women victims of violence

Giuseppe Stanziano, Adele Nunziante Cesàro[1]

The context of the intervention: some cues for possible theoretical references

We wish to introduce the reader to some observations regarding a clinical experience that took place at the "Sportello Donna" (a woman's help centre) set up in the eastern area of Naples by the Le Kassandre association, in collaboration with the PhD degree in Gender Studies at the University of Naples Federico II. The Sportello Donna provides women in various predicaments with short-term psychological consultations. In particular, it takes charge of victims of physical and psychological violence, particularly those who are subjected to intra-family abuse, that is to say, when the aggressor is actually the partner of the victim.

The geographic area in which the intervention is carried out is strongly defined by social and cultural degradation, a lack of social welfare services and the overwhelming presence of organized crime. In some of the cases under treatment, this territorial specificity has defined the whole frame in which the intervention itself has been carried out. Indeed, the offer of psychological consultation itself has sometimes appeared to be at risk, since this has been perceived by the clients as a space where words have precious little value when it comes to facing emergency situations, characterized by a concrete affectivity in which actions are rapid and volatile.

The possibility of setting up a psychological intervention able to suspend the enactment, in order to make up a framework within which the word is the means to convey thoughts and feelings, has sometimes appeared to be problematic, thereby leading the psychologists involved to rethink the sense of the inter-

---

1 The writing of this article has been carried out by both the authors equally.

vention. Moreover, with regards to those situations where the enactment and physical violence occupied a central place in the predicament of these women, the possibility of listening and turning thoughts into words sometimes appeared to the clients of the service to be an incomprehensible luxury, especially when compared to their personal situations where, on the contrary, physical violence was crystallized as a frequent behavioural praxis and a recurring modality for discharging feelings and evacuating psychic contents.

The psychological consultation is free for every client who requests it and is structured as four sessions overall, which take place at the district headquarters of Naples. In some of the cases in question, and upon the explicit request of the client, the consultations have been followed by a period of prolonged psychological support. Some of the static and constant elements characterizing the setting – such as space, times and some of the formal aspects denoting the relationship between client and psychologist – have sometimes been put under strain. This has taken the shape of repeated requests for moving forward the time or changing the place where the sessions were supposed to take place, as well as attempts to involve other subjects in the private space of the interviews between client and psychologist. The cultural and social dimensions of the whole context of the intervention, and the specificity of these requests for help, which were signified by the presence of subjected physical violence, have often challenged the material and symbolic boundaries of the setting, thereby making it particularly arduous for the mistreated women to set up the right conditions for listening and creating a space for reflection.

Regarding the tools used, other than the interviews, which have been conducted by a psychoanalytic-oriented clinical psychologist, the clients have been asked, on their second session, to undergo the TAT projective test, and have been promised feedback at the end of the consultations, after a thorough analysis of the material, supervised by an expert in projective tests. In all cases, the users accepted the administration of the TAT test.

The premises for these interviews, which involve some of the distinctive characteristics of the context of this intervention, call forth, at least in some aspects that we shall describe soon, an often talked about concept in literature – the "acting out". First and foremost, we need to outline two accepted definitions of this term; one is more extended, whereas the other is more restrictive and refers to the specificity of the psychoanalytic setting. The latter, in fact, tends to consider the acting out as an enactment that is directly linked to the transference relationship, although acted "outside" the analytic situation. According to the former definition, the "out" is instead understood as something externalized, outside of the intra-psychic. This defensive manner of expression represents an impulsive feature and assumes a specific heuristic value, as it demonstrates a recurring and isolated characteristic that considers the enactment in question as having a partial break from the usual behavioural practices of the subject. In that sense, it bears a mark of exceptionality that characterizes this defence in a unique way.

Therefore, with regards to the issues of the context of this intervention, the conceptual indication proposed here could appear inappropriate, since we do not intend to discuss how isolated enactments take place with a specific reference to the acting out. However, we have decided to refer to this construct since it brings the relationships between thought, word and action to the foreground. Indeed, considering the specificity of the following case story and the reference to the contextual indications, which will be described soon, these appear to be key elements. One of the challenges posed by acting out lies in the nature of its relationship with communication; there is, indeed, a continuum that goes from the semiotic symbolic function of the motor and sensory representation to verbalization (Ferraro & Nunziante Cesàro, 1985, p. 96). The theoretical reference frame here is the psychoanalytic Freudian discourse, which posits a psychic continuity; thus, psychic manifestations are linked with unconscious nexuses, and are overdetermined by the underlying drive impulses that move them.

What we intend to highlight here, more than the specificity of the single action-based behaviours present – whether in terms of socio-cultural dynamics which, broadly speaking, have characterized our intervention or, sometimes, in terms of the singularity of the intra-psychic processes brought into play – is a more general tendency towards acting as a way of "bringing into action" by means of motor skills.

We believe that it would be useful to take into account some considerations regarding acting out according to which, this *tends to eliminate and not regulate anxiety as well as maintain a state of not-integration, which hinders the recognition and organization of an internal space* (ibidem, p. 99). Andrè Green (1990) defines acting out as an *acted expulsion*, which determines a sort of *psychic blindness* in which the subject *loses sight of its internal reality* (ibidem, p. 67).

In this sort of breaking down between internal and external reality, we witness an overinvestment of the network with short and rapid social actions aimed at eclipsing the internal world. Moreover, we would like to underline some indications of the acting out proposed by Laplanche and Pontalis (1967), which is outlined by its characteristics of being both self- and hetero-aggressive. This brings us back to the issue of physical violence, which we have already touched upon.

The sensitive hub around which violent actions turn is represented by the body, which constitutes the elective place on which to exercise violence (Ferraro, 2009), since the forms of physical violence, imply a "breaking hit" into the body's boundaries. This definition of violent manifestation implies thinking about the body and its link with psychic processes, which act to represent and give shape to the unconscious contents that characterize the psychic world.

The body can be simultaneously understood both as a starting point and as a driving force of symbolizations, in that psychism shows its profound root through the soma as a means of the translation of body-bound instinctual impulses, and as an instrument of de-symbolization by means of the modalities of discharging through the body drive impulses which, lacking a representational configuration, make their way through a closely somatic-bound discharge. Within this theoretical frame, physical violence appears to be a deficit of symbolization – that is, *a symbolic minus in which a destructive action constitutes the extreme or, at the very least, the last expressive option available* (Garella, 2009, p.16). With regards to these theoretical references, the terms under discussion here – which would seem to be useful for defining some of the contextual specificities described above – are: violence, the body and symbolization. This is a conceptual triad, imbued with theoretical issues that assume an explanatory value for the specificity of our context of intervention.

With particular reference to dictatorial political situations, Argentine psychoanalysis has been interested in cases in which a menace (Puget, 1989) invades one's psychological space and comes to control the times and forms of the listening, just like an insurmountable *diktat* that puts a strain on the possibilities of the thought. Given this frame, it is necessary to cogently take into account the link between internal and external reality (Nunziante Cesàro, 1994) – that is, the link between a socio-cultural world, which is always present (although here it shows an overwhelming presence), and the subject's intra-psychic world. The menace described by Puget shows a violence that exists permanently, both as a real possibility always lurking around, and as an imaginary feature, which takes the shape of internal representations. The feeling of constant uncertainty and of an invasion of the psyche from past experiences of danger determines the awkward anxieties that paralyse the activity of thought. Although the author herself notes that a similar state of affairs, albeit quite extreme, is observed in social and political situations not necessarily as extreme as those experienced by 1970s Argentina, we do not intend to compare them *tout court* to our context of the intervention. Here, in fact, legality is nonetheless guaranteed, although this is somewhat at risk considering that we are in a territory marked by a strong Camorra[2] presence.

At any rate, the above-mentioned considerations have appeared to provide a precious reference when it comes to thinking over some of the sequences extrapolated from our clinical experience. For instance, some of our patients would leave their homes and head straight towards the premises of the interviews, lest they be assaulted. Sometimes, the interviews themselves have been interrupted by relatives, who suddenly turn up to

---

2   Camorra is a crime organization actives in Italy.

"check things out", or by the "escape" of the client, who had been alarmed by an anonymous phone call.

The psychoanalyst Wilfred Bion's reflection upon the common saying "actions speak louder than words" shows an acknowledgment of the power of a "language of achievement" (1970), used to eliminate the word. In this scenario, the value of facts imposes itself as the only effectively substantial reality, causing every attempt aimed at creating a mental space – understood as a possibility for thought to take in uncertainty and tolerate doubt and the unknown – to be fruitless. According to Bion, there are two fundamental features that drive listening: *patience*, which is understood as the capacity to await the discourse taking shape, *without getting anxious by facts and reasons described* (ibidem p. 168), and *self-confidence*, which evokes a sense of protection and a decrease in anxiety. When these two conditions appear to be put under particular strain by a traumatic, immediate, and emergency-related effectiveness, the passage to action would seem to be a favoured modality for evacuating anxiety while sacrificing the functions of the thought.

In the light of the theoretical contributions proposed here, the question we set out to raise concerns the conditions under which it is possible to carry out a short-term psychological intervention while facing violence-related situations in a context marked by the pre-eminence of action over thought. All of which begs the question: "What possibilities are there, both in terms of the socio-cultural context and with reference to the specificity of intra-psychic processes, for beneficial psychological listening in conditions in which there is less space for the functions of the thought and the capacities of elaborating them through words?" With regards to this, we realized that administrating the TAT test could turn out to be an unexpected resource (over and above the diagnostic contribution that this test already brings about), as this puts the subject's ability for symbolizing to the test while showing to the tested subject themselves the limits and difficulties of their own modalities of psychic elaboration.

Methodological assumptions of the TAT test

The Thematic Apperception Test is a projective instrument created by Mugan and Murray in 1935. Its first version included 20 pictures that featured different scenes about which the subject was asked to tell a story. The most historically important contribution to psychoanalytic projective methodologies, which provides a more structured conceptual and methodological setting that opens up the way to experimentation, was made in the 1960s by ego psychology (Rapaport, Gill & Shafer, 1968), which had the merit of turning the focus of attention from *the contents to the container* (Brelet, 1986) – in other words, the clinician's attention is focused on the process dynamics that the subject brings into play in order to confer the visual scene with a perceived re-presentation and dramatization.

Moreover, in the 1960s in France, Vica Schentoub (Schentoub et al., 1990) began a long and profitable reflection over projective techniques, which led her to conceive an evaluative model of the TAT test, centred upon the forms and features of the fantasmatic investment. According to this perspective, the subject's imaginative production is stimulated by the vision of the cards, which put their capacity for cathexis to the test while keeping them at a good distance from the fantasy evoked.

Therefore, through these procedures, which have acquired a specific formulation over time, it is possible to evaluate the permeability of the subject's psychical structure and the dynamics of their primary and secondary processes.

The TAT test triggers a process of psychic elaboration – that is, the "TAT process". This is developed in three phases, to wit:

1) The first phase is perceptive; the subject looks at the cards and makes an initial perceptive selection, according to the internal resonance that the pictures stimulate.

2) The second phase requires an integration of these solicitations. This implies a psychic process to bind the drive, in order to contain it in a possible representation of affect.

3) The third phase is creative. By achieving a secondary elaboration-based word-presentation, the narration conveys the movement of drive activated by regression.

The evaluative criteria of the psychical movements described above are based on the modalities and level of secondary processes. Therefore, elements that provide an index for understanding the story are factors such as: the legibility of the story as a possibility of being a shareable experience; the temporal pace of the narration; the richness or inadequacy of the description; coherence; flexibility; and narrative dynamicity.

Moreover, the creation of an explicative grid, which is readjusted and re-elaborated over time, represents the attempt to make the procedure of evaluating the story more formal and shareable, through a common evaluation of the psychic dynamics in the carrying out of the TAT process.

With reference to the metapsychological considerations of the projective process, the aspects more profitable for our discourse about those contexts and psychical processes that are marked by a tendency to use enactments lie within an economical perspective; this has a key role in that it calls forth the matters of the intensity of excitement and the movements of drive impulses when these undergo a process of transformation. In this regard, the TAT process puts the very fantasmatic[3] activity to the test (Brelet, 1986) – in other words, the psychical work necessary to bind the drive impulse and contain it within the forms of symbolization. In this sense, the attention paid to the modalities of translation and the figuration of drive impulses requires a reflection upon the overflowing and uncontrollable aspects of the cathexis energy or, on the contrary, upon the poverty and misery when we are in the presence of withdrawal and decathexis.

The projective situation can be thought of as a relational dynamic, in which it is possible to see three elements in action, simultaneously interacting with one another, namely the subject, the clinician and the TAT test. The development of this relational setting implies a substantial amount of cathexis, with a displacement of feelings and representation moving around the vertices of this relationship. In this light, the individuality of the projective setting is imprinted within the clinical transference (Chabert, 1998), as it implies a translation of internal psychical phenomena onto the external reality.

The projective situation, as described with reference to the three vertices of the relational field, brings into bear different transference-based phenomena. On one hand, the TAT test shows a concrete (tough, ambiguous) material, in this way stimulating a double level of cathexis – that is, per-ceptive and fantasmatic. On the other hand, the clinician, as a guarantor of the rule (Brelet, 1986), is not meant to judge, and should maintain a neutral and self-restrained stance in order to let the subject create associations and, in so doing, become themselves the object of possible cathexis.

The third vertex is represented by the subject, who is spurred to oscillate between manifest content, and the possibility of letting their thoughts formally regress. The projective situation is part and parcel of a transference relation, in which the mediator object – that is, the card – steers and binds translation.

The evaluation of the associative material produced is, basically, the analysis of the discourse processes brought to bear in elaborating the story. In this kind of analysis, the primary reference frame is the psychoanalytic clinical thought, according to which the relationships with the metapsychological dis-course and with the difference between primary and secondary processes, and the repartition between neurotic, psychotic and borderline mental functioning, are central.

However, the idea of the heterogeneity of psychic functioning implies yielding the structural perspective to a vision more concerned with the processes of psychic dynamics. In this sense, Chabert (2011) points out that every diagnosis – or at least those elaborated by dint of those projective methodologies consistent with this school of thought – is a differential diagnosis. With

---

3   The psychoanalytic notion of "fantasmatic" – or "phantasmatic", as sometimes it is written – refers to psychic capability to transform perceptions and excitements in mental representations.

regards to the use of the TAT test in the above-mentioned counselling setting, the latter is aimed at achieving a diagnostic evaluation which, although always present, is nonetheless intentionally left in the background, rather than deepening the knowledge of possible psychical processes that is gained though this projective instrument, and discussed as well as questioned with the client during the consultations.

The discourse analysis produced by the subject facing the TAT test focuses mainly on the oscillation between primary and secondary processes – in other words, on the capacity of the subject to place themselves at a good *distance* (Brelet, 1986) from the card under examination. This calls forth the capacity to have access to a fantasmatic resonance, which by fostering the discursive production, undergoes a secondary revision. In this sense, the quality and intensity of the fantasmatic solicitations, the symbolic depth of ability to articulate the wish and defence dynamics, and the quality of the figurative work all become the objects of evaluation.

The creation of an interpretative grid serves the purpose not only of facilitating the interpretation of the material brought by the subject, but also of providing the necessary criteria to formalize and orientate the assessment. Although these criteria are decided by the same clinician involved in the process and then supervised, they become, in this way, shareable and reciprocally verified. Therefore, the interpretative grid must be seen as an occupational tool, able to provide a possible overall vision of the complexity inherent in the psychical dynamics under examination. The grid is also constantly checked and readjusted according to the indications provided by the clinical practice, which, in our view, always exceeds every exhaustive attempt at definition.

The grid put forth by Chabert and Brelet (2003) divides the organization of psychical processes into four series:

The first two series, called "A" and "B", refer to some of the processes of discourse analysis that are typical of neurotic functioning. In this case, there is an intense internal cathexis and relevant intra-psychic conflicts, which can take two different modalities of expression, namely an obsessive-type modality of thought, with regards to series A, and an interpersonal, relationships-based and dramatization-oriented modality, with regards to series B.

Series C is characterized by an avoidance of the conflict – that is to say, a modality of decathexis from fantasmatic solicitations, along with a rather poor internal resonance. Characteristically associated with this series, therefore, are some body-bound modalities for expressing drive impulses or a strong adhesion to perception aimed at paralysing cathexis. The processes underlying series C are generally present in all the modalities of psychical functioning. However, in the case of a straightforward pervasiveness, they can call forth characteristics that are relevant to borderlines.

Series E encompasses modalities of thought whose primary processes are particularly intense and overflowing from the perimeter of the secondary process work. Although they do not necessarily refer to psychotic modalities of psychical functioning, they nonetheless show a possible hypercathexis of archaic fantasies.

The case of Mariagrazia: some considerations of a clinical case

We wish to report some of the elements extrapolated from the story of one of our patients, in order to show some significant clinical sequences related to the administration and analysis of the TAT test.

Mariagrazia is a 26-year-old woman who, about 20 days before the interview, sued her cohabitee for physical violence. The police gave her the number of the help centre where I am meeting her for a supportive psychological interview; it was her mother who called me to arrange an appointment. Mariagrazia asks me not to say anything to her mother of what she is about to tell me during the interviews. She also warns me against possible telephone calls coming from her mother, aimed at asking for news about her. Piecing together her story is not an easy task, as it consists of many escapes and moves around Italy, many lovers, and the violence to which she has been subjected coming both from her family and her partners.

Mariagrazia had her first son when she was 14 years old. She says that she longed for this child; in fact, she conceived him with her former boyfriend, hoping that her mother would accept her relationship with this man. She says that she has always wished for a house, a husband with a job, and children – "something normal," she adds. Her second child was conceived with another man. Mariagrazia has had many short-term and intense relationships one after another, and with men she meets in the street or on the Internet. Her mother and brother often lock her in their house, so Mariagrazia has run away on many occasions, sometimes interrupting her relationship with her family for a few months, but rejoined them eventually.

The previous summer, after her mother found out that she was pregnant again, her brother beat her and so she escaped, again running several kilometres away. Over the following days, she had a miscarriage. While telling this story, she cries desperately.

She has not seen her father for years. The last time she met him, it was only for half an hour and in a secret place, since her father is a fugitive and most likely a member of the Camorra. Unlike her brother, who hates his father, she misses him dearly and she says that sooner or later she wants to meet him again.

Her mother is engaged in a new relationship with another man – a "good man, he is not my father though". Mariagrazia wants to take back the accusation made against her partner, who is a drug user, because he does not deserve it. They have recently gotten in touch again by telephone; Maria-grazia says that she loves him and that "this time things are different". After all, "this" – he beat and left her with wounds and contusions, because they had a silly argument – has happened only "three" times since they started to cohabit around a year ago.

Mariagrazia confides that she has not been able to keep herself awake over the past few days. Her mother does not allow her to do anything, not even to talk on the telephone; therefore, she can do nothing but sleep. The day before the interview, she slept for 24 hours in a row, locked in her bedroom; she cannot tolerate noise, and prefers to be alone in the dark.

These are the interviews in summary. If we turn our attention to the data that emerged from the administration of the TAT test, we notice a straight-forward predominance of the processes referring to series C. These, in fact, show, through different complex clinical manifestations and psychical processes, a psychic dynamic intended to avoid and inhibit the affective elements stimulated by the pictures. Since the latter lack an efficient representative and symbolic content, they appear flattened against purely factual feelings. And yet, along with predominant modalities apparently close to enactment and the passage to the act of feelings, there is the concomitant presence of a significant intra-psychic cathexis, which can be seen as a positive indicator for the trans-formative process of the elaboration of feelings.

The request to make up a story starting from the cards, albeit positively and collaboratively taken up, put a strain on the subject when it came for her to develop a representation able to contain her affective solicitations. What is striking, in our opinion, is that these difficulties, and the inhibition and dis-ability they bring with them, have been not only observed through the projective instrument, but also felt by the subject herself when under examination.

- When faced with the fifth card, which, with regards to the codified latent content, refers to an overbearing and controlling female/maternal figure, Mariagrazia says: *I don't know... perhaps during these two days when I wanted to stay alone in my bedroom... I get this feeling... No, un-fortunately I always act instinctively so I can't think about anything. My mother who opens up the door 'cause she doesn't get when someone wants to stay on her own... I hate light! Enough, I'm stuck.*

From the analyses of the data gained through the afore-mentioned grid, it is possible to draw the following conclusions: the elaboration times appear long, and are characterized by a tendency for refusal. It is also possible to observe both different and heterogeneous modalities of functioning, which appear to characterize the whole discourse. In other words, it is possible to identify an oscillation between a representative register, which seems lacking, and a sensorial and impressions-based register. The contingent reference to her personal experience is central, and assumes depressive and withdrawal modalities.

- When faced with the first card, which features a thoughtful child who is looking at a violin, Mariagrazia says: *When my brother used to go to middle school, he would enjoy playing, and then he gave up, not the violin though, the piano. It made me think about my brother. What a strange thing, a picture can make you think about something out of its context. All of a sudden things you never think about pop into your mind.*

The card immediately brings out a personal memory, in which the representation-bound latent intra-psychic conflict is present. The personal reference seems to be central. It is, in fact, restated and it also overwhelms the dynamic itself. In that sense, the sensation of surprise expressed by this woman appears remarkable; she seems almost amazed by the insurgence of an internal representation deriving from her visual perception.

- When faced with the card numbered 9GF, which features two women who are running on two different levels, Mariagrazia says (getting closer to the card): *I don't get the place, the people in it. I can't... are these two different women or is it still the same one? I can't even understand what kind of place this is, the point where they are, is it a break in the ground there? It's like it's broken here. Perhaps there are some leaves... I don't know. This card just brought panic out of me, I mean the Modena thing, the earthquake, I've got some relatives in Modena. My stomach just lurched.*

At the end of the test administration, Mariagrazia asks why she is not able to imagine or fantasize about anything; she says that she is concerned about that. She says that she has tried so hard to imagine how to tell the stories, even though she simply had to make them up, as was suggested to her several times, but it was like she "no longer had anything in her mind". Over the following interviews, the discourse, still referring to the projective test, turned around the feeling of not being able to think and the capacity to tell actions, feelings and thoughts apart. By virtue of this "experience", which seems to have particularly involved her, and with the support of the psychologist, Mariagrazia tries to think over some extracts from the previous interviews. In particular, she asks herself how much she has really chosen the things that have happened to her. At the fourth interview, as was explained to her at the beginning, she opts for the opportunity to continue with the consultations. She says that getting out of her house to attend the interviews is the only chance for her to stop sleeping and get out of the dark room.

Mariagrazia attends weekly interviews, which bring out moments of intense sadness in which she says feel like having lost everything and not having any hope left of getting anything good out of life. About a month after the beginning of the interviews, Mariagrazia telephones to let the psychologist know that she has decided to leave and go to a northern Italian city, where one of her cousins lives. This is a sudden and unexpected decision, which is unlikely to have taken any space within the previous interviews to be expressed or thought through and, as such, appears to be another possible escape.

In conclusion, we believe that the dynamic of physical violence implies a double relational aspect – that is, the violent action perpetrated by the aggressor and the victim's body violation. In both cases, it is possible to track the aspect of de-symbolization that the violence brings about: the aggressor confers a concrete efficacy to his action, which goes beyond the forms of the thought and symbolization, while the victims concretely experience the traumatic break on their body. Although in some contexts a certain "tolerance" to physical violence is thought to exist, like a sort of habituation to beatings, we believe that the universal traumatic effect that this shows, as a painful break of one's body boundaries, is an inescapable fact.

References

Bion, Wilfred (1970). *Attention and interpretation,* London: Tavistock Pubblications, tr. it, *Attenzione e interpretazione*, Armando editore, 1992.

Brelet-Foulard, Francoise (1986). *Il T.A.T. Fantasma e situazione proiettiva*, RaffaelloCortina Editore, Milano 1994.

Brelet-Foulard, Francoise & Chabert, Catherine (2003). (a cura di) *Nouveau Manuel du TAT*, Dunod, Parigi.

Chabert, Catherine (1998). *Psicoanalisi e metodi proiettivi*, Borla, Milano 2006.

Chabert, Catherine (2011). appunti del corso: *Diagnostic differentiel en psychopathologie de l'enfant, de l'adolescent et de l'adulte. Approche clinique et projective.* 19 – 23 settembre 2011, Institute de Psychologie, Universite Paris Descartes – Paris V.

Ferraro, Fausta (2009). *Linee d'ombra e di confine: vertici psicoanalitici per una riflessione*, in "Violenza e simbolizzazione", a cura di A. Garella e R. Musella, Ed. La Bilbioteca, Bari.

Ferraro, Fausta & Nunziante Cesàro, Adele (1985). *Lo spazio cavo e il corpo saturato*, FrancoAngeli, Milano.

Garella, Alessandro (2009). *Violenza e simbolizzazione*, in "Violenza e simbolizzazione", a cura di A. Garella e R. Musella, Ed. La Bilbioteca, Bari.

Green, André (1990). *La follia privata. Psicoanalisi degli stati limite*, Cortina Ed., Milano 1991.

Green, André (1973), *Il discorso vivente. La concezione psicoanalitica dell'affetto*, Astrolabio, Roma 1974.

Green, André (2002), *La pensée clinique*, Editions Odile Jacobs, Parigi.

Laplanche, Jean & Pontalis, Jean Baptiste (1967). *Enciclopedia della psicoanalisi*. Bari, Laterza, 1984.

Nunziante Cesàro Adele (1994). *Prefazione all'edizione italiana*, in "Violenza di stato e psicoanalisi", Guido Gnocchetti Ed., Napoli, 1994.

Nunziante Cesàro Adele, Stanziano Giuseppe, Riccardi Elisabetta (2012). *La rana e lo scorpione. Percorsi di autonomia e differenziazione per le donne vittime di violenze*, in Caterina Arcidiacono, Imma Di Napoli, (a cura di), "Sono caduta dalle scale ... I luoghi e gli attori della violenza di genere", FrancoAngeli, Milano.

Puget, Janine (1989). Stato di minaccia e psicoanalisi, in "Violenza di stato e psicoanalisi", Guido Gnocchetti Ed., Napoli, 1994.

Shentoub, Vica & Al. (1990). *Manuel d'utilisation du T.A.T.*, Dunot, Parigi.

Sommantico, Massimiliano (2006). *Introduzione all'edizione italiana, in C. Chabert Psicoanalisi e metodi proiettivi*, Borla, Roma.

The experience of domestic violence: an interpretative-phenomenological analysis

Mihaela Dana Bucuță, Gabriela Dima

Introduction and context

Domestic violence became a topic of public debate in Romania only after 1995. Following the end of communist regime (after 1989), one of the main problems of the country was children in care. The study of this situation started with an analysis of the causes of child abandonment and has led to issues related to families facing social problems. A complex and ample phenomenon has arisen which had to be inevitably recognized, that of domestic violence.

Intervention possibilities were limited at that time, as the Romanian Criminal Code did not include family violence as a distinct offence. In 2003, 33 non-governmental organizations had come together to combat and prevent family violence and founded the National Coalition of NGO's involved in Programs on Violence against Women. The first specific legislation on domestic violence enacted in 2003[1] was followed by a national strategy for prevention and combating of domestic violence during 2005–2007.[2]

Following these legislative initiatives, a body of research and literature on the topic of family violence emerged. Domestic violence is defined as a repeated series of coercive behaviours and physical, sexual and psychological assault, manifested by a person toward his/her partner, in order to control and dominate him/her, using force and/or taking advantage of the victim's incapacity for defence, which appears in a couple relationships. Economic and social abuses are included. It is considered domestic violence also when committed against a former wife / partner and within consensual relationships (Centrul de Resurse Juridice și Institutul de Cercetare și Prevenire a Criminalității, 2003).

---

1   Law 217/2003 on preventing and combating family violence. Published in the Official Monitor no. 678, 25 May, 2005.
2   Decision 686/2005 for approval of the National Strategy in the field of preventing and combating family violence. Published in the Official Monitor no. 367, 29 May, 2003.

The first large-scale research was the *"National study on family and workplace violence"* conducted in 2003 by the Centre Partnership for Equality on a randomly stratified sample of 1806 people representative of the Romanian adult population (over 18 years, (excluding those institutionalized). Conclusions draw attention to the alarming dimensions of the phenomenon of violence both within family and at work:

- compared to statistics of the European Union, Romanian population is significantly more tolerant towards domestic violence in all its forms;

- high tolerance together with the use of clichés about violence lead to considering violent behaviour as normal behaviour;

- disguised as normal, violent behaviour is transmitted from one generation to another.

As most Romanian studies looked at domestic violence especially in terms of statistics, the present study proposes an inside view of the phenomenon by giving voice and making sense of the experience of women subjected to domestic violence. This is considered to be a prerequisite to calibrate interventions in the field.

Methodology

The study design is qualitative and the method used is Interpretative Phenomenological Analysis (IPA), chosen for its potential to bring an in-depth understanding of the lived experiences of women victims of domestic violence. The underlying assumption is that interventions have to be grounded in the meaning that women give to their life experiences.

The method of the Interpretative Phenomenological Analysis (IPA) was introduced by Jonathan A. Smith (Smith, 1996) in the field of health psychology. IPA can be described by three broad elements: an epistemological position, guidelines for conducting research and a corpus of empirical research (Smith, 2004). The term *"interpretative phenomenological analysis"* signals the dual nature of the approach (Smith, 1996): the phenomenological requirement to understand and *"give voice,"* exploring the participant's inside view on the phenomenon under study, and the interpretative requirement to contextualise and *"make sense"* of these claims from a psychological perspective (Larkin, Watts & Clifton, 2006). Hence, IPA implies a *"double hermeneutic:"* participants making sense of their personal and social world, and the researcher trying to make sense of the participants' sense-making of their world (Smith & Osborn, 2008).

IPA studies are usually concerned with existential issues such as significant *"life transforming or life threatening"* moments (Smith, 2004) and is suitable to respond to broadly and openly framed research questions (Smith & Osborn, 2008).

The research questions of this study are: How do women victims of domestic violence experience abuse? How do they make sense of the abuse? How does abuse affect them?

IPA uses small sample sizes, Brocki & Wearden's meta-analyses (2006) show ranges from one single case up to a number of 35 participants, selected mainly by purposive sampling as broadly homogenous samples. This study included a sample of 8 abused women aged 23 to 56, with different social and professional backgrounds, which experienced domestic violence over a minimum of one year. Data were collected using phenomenological interviews and analysed with IPA.

Findings

The Interpretative Phenomenological Analysis has led to a matrix of five themes: *"living with violence," "identity: I before versus I now," "coping with violence," "Me and the world," "Myself... I am a failure".*

The first theme, *"Living with the violence"* reflects the experience of abused women. All study participants refer to the decision to marry. A world of dreams and desires marked the beginning of the marriage. That whole world collapsed with the first time they were beaten. A surprising and shocking moment they did not know how to face. The first punch has been followed by countless others of greater intensity and severity. All the participants talked about experiences of extreme physical violence: *"You think you can die anytime. You cannot breathe anymore under a storm of punches, shots in the abdomen ... you really cannot breathe at all..."* says Ioana.[3] Physical abuse is always accompanied by psychological abuse *"he swore, he was saying I was good for nothing"* and many times by sexual abuse *"does not even matter if I want to make love to him... if he wants... we do. I think I preferred to do what he says... because I feared that... he would force me to... and to make me do it"* (Cristina).

The experience of violence can't be understood and makes no sense. The women try to find an explanation for this inhuman behaviour, sometimes invoking insanity, sometimes alcohol, but they fail to contain the experience in all its violence: *"he acts like an animal, because he acts instinctively, and perhaps not even so. Animals do not attack if they are not in danger. What*

---

3   All names are changed for confidentiality and anonymity reasons

kind of danger can he feel next to a woman who has only loved him? Next to a child that all he does is to jump into his arms?" (Maria)

The women's lives are marked by sadness, fear, discouragement, helplessness and despair. Finally, life doesn't make sense *"my life has no logic, no course"* (Maria).

The second theme *"Identity"* shows how the violence experience changes the women. All of them, without exception, talked about a profound change in their nature: *"It hurts me that I've turned into something I never thought I'll be. I turned into... something I did not want, something I hate to be"* (Angela).

The third theme *"Coping with Violence"* shows how their whole life becomes a continuous defence. They all learned to avoid, anticipating in order to avoid beatings. Of course, the strategy does not work well because the outbreaks of violence have no logic. Sometimes the refuge is in domestic activities, sometimes the children can be a support, a motivation to resist, but even these strategies are not all efficient. Even if all women said they feel hate for the husband when they are abused, only one of them fought back physically.

"Me and the World" treats the theme of social network and social support. All women talked about a progressive withdrawal from social relationships. If initially the withdrawal was a way to deal with violence by the same attempt to reduce the risk of further beatings, with time passing the avoidance and rejection occurred mainly due to the feelings of shame and fear of being judged. The women's whole lives began to take place "behind closed doors". Isolation, loneliness, hopelessness and lack of trust in people seal their lives. The corollary is that behind closed doors, the woman that experience domestic violence is living her tragedy convinced that she is a failure. This is the main theme of the paper and highlights the consequences of domestic violence as they are experienced by abused women. It is an inside view.

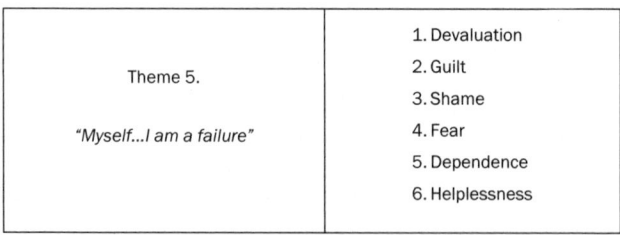

Theme 5.	1. Devaluation
	2. Guilt
	3. Shame
"Myself...I am a failure"	4. Fear
	5. Dependence
	6. Helplessness

Table 1.The theme "Myself… I am a failure"

1. Depreciation / humiliation "Only one slap... it makes you feel worthless"

For all women the first time being hit is experienced as a shock: "*I just could not believe. Everything was so fast. Only one slap... it makes you feel worthless*" (Roxana). This remains as an unforgettable landmark moment and marks the beginning of a life nightmare: "*I can't ever forget that day. As they say, then began my end as woman, as wife*" said Roxana.

Physical violence, verbal and sexual violence deeply injures women's identity and dignity: "*you feel the lowest human being. I felt the last human being... not even a dog is hit as I was. Battered... I couldn't hope for anything, I was not waiting for tomorrow anymore*" (Maria).

Emotional abuse leaves deep scars: "*he still criticizes me because I gained weight and he says he no longer wants me and... he makes me ashamed of myself, of how I look... I think this hurt more than his slaps*" (Roxana).

The loss of self-value is felt in all life areas: "*This statute... I do not have it anymore... I am not even appreciated for my work, what to say about the other qualities... devalued is not the word... where is my self-esteem, my esteem as a woman... not by a long shot*" (Cristina). Finally she acknowledges "*I feel that... I am no longer good for anything, I am not worth anything ... I feel empty inside*".

When these women think of their lives they are dominated by an acute sense of failure: "*I feel I am a real failure. A failure for him, for me as a woman... now a failure even professionally*" (Cristina).

2. Guilt "I had to know... it's my fault"

All women feel guilt about the situation of abuse, just the forms of its manifestation differs. Angela's guilt is related to her level of education, which, although high was not helpful for fighting with violence: "*Me, after studying so much, I've been so close minded, I wonder what about those poor country girls, what they feel like and how they accept all this*". Ioana's guilt is due to her weakness and inability to handle the situation even if "*I was hospitalised two weeks, broken arm... I woke up, I did not even know where I was... I have been a coward*". Diana, who eventually managed to gather the strength to leave the situation of abuse, feels bad because she didn't do it earlier: "*I let myself be threatened too long... too much... that he would kill me, that if I divorce he takes Nati away from me, that he would set fire to the house... I didn't care about the house or anything else*".

Pain and guilt are even greater when children are in the middle: "*The first thing I think about is that... I gave my daughter the worst father. I am guilty for that and I'm ashamed of myself*" (Diana).

3. Shame

Guilt is closely linked to the shame, as Roxana shows: *"Yes, I've got away from it all because I didn't want to give them explanations anymore. It's shameful. It's embarrassing because you know it's only your fault. But when you do it with your hand... You should be... you should feel shame!"* In addition, there is the belief that others will criticize, judge and condemn: *"You can read it on their faces... It seems they shout: 'you are guilty', 'Who made you', 'that's what you deserve'... and yes... that's what I deserve".* This is the moment when social isolation creeps in: *"You think I don't feel guilty? You think I want to see their judgemental faces? Yes!!! That's why I got away from them. I want to be left alone"* (Roxana).

The feelings of shame appear in relation to all the important persons: *"I was ashamed of colleagues, didn't want him to make a scene in front of them"*; *"I feel ashamed in front of my parents... We had made fools of ourselves enough with the yelling. Neighbours, friends, they all knew us... downright awful"* (Roxana).

4. Fear "Living with this fear... your soul is shaking"

The moments when the partner becomes aggressive, violent and threatening causes immense fear, which is difficult to master: *"I was scared, terrified even. I did not know anything else but that I had to escape from his fury. Didn't know why... I fell asleep locked in the bathroom that night. I cried all night while he was yelling across the door and threatening me with death"* (Denisa). The threats are terrifying, directed either directly to the woman or to her loved ones: *"he threatened to kill them if I would leave him; he threatened me that day that if I tell someone about what happened, he will catch me alone and then..."* (Roxana). But the fear not only accompanies the episodes of abuse, it is continuous, that fear of not knowing what will happen next: *"I am terrified. Yes ... I'm so afraid because I don't know what will happen next to him. I have no security... you know how it feels?... It feels like hell. You are like a defenceless child... alone in the world... you cannot live peacefully because you have to lookout for something that can happen anytime. Everything is ok and suddenly bang a slap behind the neck..."* (Cristina).

The fear continues even after the separation from her husband.

5. Dependence

As time passes, the critical words, humiliation, degrading words that the husband has thrown on the woman lead her to doubt her own judgment: *"he says things that maybe are not true, and... you get to believe them... and... you lose faith in you"* (Maria). As she says, the loss is even larger; it is lack of confidence in your own, in others, and in life: *"I cannot trust anyone, not even myself...".*

Personal power is surrendered in the hands of the abuser husband and this marks the annihilation of being of the woman. The abuser has the right of life and death over his wife: *"I give him the decision right. I gave him veto power in terms of my professional, social, intimate life... I have no control over my life. I have no freedom... I cannot decide... cannot take a decision..."* (Maria). The incapacity to take decisions leads to dependence on others. The stronger dependence is the one related to the abuser husband and is the most difficult to overcome. Diana is one of the women aware of psychological dependence of her husband and managed to get away from him: *"Hate, despair, physical and mental helplessness... it was more psychological addiction. The preconceived idea that without him I will not be able to raise Nati, but I realized that a child should not bind you to a brutal, violent man that just beats you down... I want to be independent again".*

6. Helplessness "It's too late for me"

Violence deprives the woman of her personal power "I felt so helpless in the face of his anger..." (Angela).

Faced with repeated violence, women feel trapped, with no possibility to escape from these cycles as is the case with Cristina, subdued by ambivalence: *"A part of me knows what is to be done, but it doesn't... a part of me wants... but it is too afraid to implement. Another part doesn't know and... I do not know what to do. I want to be happy but it's hard to give up everything I have now... I cannot take it over again. It's too much for me. I do not feel able to do it".*

All this marks the capitulation of the woman: *"I am no longer good for anything. I'm too depressed to take the initiative of a change... but I mean it: I can't anymore. I cannot ... what to do if I can't"* (Cristina).

The failure to change something makes women feel trapped in the cycle of violence; feel that they have no future: *"For me the future is quite dark. As I said, no reason... I just don't hope anymore. I'm not dreaming..."* (Cristina).

Only the women who have left the relationship could project into the future. Diana has a clear and positive overview: *"Five years?... once I'm done with the divorce... I'll start masters, I'll open a legal office and I will help women who have experienced the same mistreatment as me".*

Roxana hopes that time will help healing after the nightmare she lived: *"I expect the time to pass... the one that is supposed to cure everything. All*

soul wounds... all the bruises... I wait for something beautiful to appear in my life, so I can enjoy it again".
Sometimes it remains *"the fear that I'll live as I lived... the fear that this time I will not be able to get up"* (Maria). For the others, the future does not exist.

Discussion

The second level of interpretation, according to the rules of interpretative phenomenological analysis (Smith & Osborn, 2008) is to attempt to give sense to the participant's reports and to link them with other results from literature. The purpose of this study was not to produce generalized findings. In order to obtain more clarity and coherence, the strategy of the Discussion's section is built on the dimensions explored in this study, emphasizing the one related to the theme *"Myself... I am a failure."*

Domestic violence experience and attributing meanings

Autobiographical construction of participants in this study provides a representation of what they were, what they are and what they could be; more precisely, what they will not be able to become.

Invited to tell their life story in brief, they all refer to their life before being abused and the life after. Regardless of age, social background, level of education and training, independently even of the abuse period (from one year for Denise to over 20 years for Angela) all the women describe domestic violence experience as one of torture. These women's lives turned into constant physical, emotional and mental pain and suffering, intentionally caused by the abusive husband, in order to punish, to intimidate and to pressure, based in all cases mostly on gender discrimination. Our results are in agreement with the OMCT report, which argues that domestic violence is a form of woman-focused torture (Benninger-Budel & Lacroix, 1999).

The first punch/slap is an autobiographical reference point. Beyond the physical pain, they all live this moment with amazement, shock; they were unprepared and surprised, they all said *"they were not expecting something like"* (Maria). Data analysis shows that this surprise effect is considered by all women included in the research group as a real trauma factor, which is similar to findings of traumatology researchers (Fisher & Riedesser, 2001).

The "surprise moment" leaves no time for the woman to put herself in position to categorize the information and to create effective plans of action. Experience of violence is unpredictable and even impossible to anticipate. A schematic state of knowledge available for abused women is not prepared for the categorization and the development of such information. Traumatic information is generally unconceivable, and that *"fills you with dread of the unknown."* (Fisher & Riedesser, 2001)

All victims reported that not only was the "first punch" a surprise; the whole domestic violence experience is retained as surprising, even if not in meaning of time. Analysis and interpretation of victims voice shows that each act of violence is unexpected and unpredictable in a different way. Women cannot imagine the amount of brutality, violence and terror they are made to face and cannot find an explanation for such behaviour coming from the one who is invested (through the act of marriage) with function to support, protect and love. This is what leads to the incapacity to give meaning to the domestic violence experience.

Losing personal value

All the women reported extreme physical violence and a preference by their abusive husbands to hit the face in particular, with the clear aim of leaving a mark. These traces have the significance of marking territory by abusers. The message is clear, the abused woman sees it: she knows who her master is. Barbaric acts of extreme violence dehumanize in equal amounts the abusive husband and the assaulted wife. Verbal and psychological violence accompanies in all cases the physical violence. Not only does the physical abuse leads to devaluation of the women but also, equally, all the other forms of abuse. Data analysis shows that victims of domestic violence relate the same sense of humiliation, of "trampling of the human condition" to psychological, sexual, social, economic, verbal and emotional abuse. All these had disastrous consequences to all women victims included in the research group, in accordance with most of available studies on domestic violence (Killen, 2003).

All women included in the group report that they were threatened, manipulated, often deprived of economic resources and relationships with others. An abusive spouse requires the victim's social isolation, even from other family members in order to avoid letting them know about the suffering. These are characteristic features for the experience of domestic violence's victims, extensively discussed in the literature (Muntean, Popescu, Marciana, Popa & Smaranda, 2000). Beaten woman syndrome (Walker, 1984) is also found in all eight cases included in the present study. For all eight stories there are general medical reports, progressive withdrawal from social relationships and isolation, physical neglect, being indifferent to the way they are seen, suicidal ideation, suicide attempts, depression, neglect and even maltreatment of children (Ioana). Data analysis shows however that all these issues must be understood in relation to the model of learned helplessness, depression, emotional and behavioural characteristics generated by cumulative exposure to violent treatment in relation to the partner.

Fear, Guilt, Shame

Fear, guilt and shame are central coordinating feelings of the lives of abused women. In five of the eight cases included in this study violent behaviour appeared before marriage. Data analysis shows that in spite of that, self-defence didn't activate itself, the woman choosing to marry the aggressor. With small exceptions, self-defence does not activate itself even after repeated violent behaviour, this being considered in literature as a characteristic of domestic violence (Muntean, Popescu, Marciana, Popa & Smaranda, 2000). In one case only (Maria) was violence answered with violence as self-defence. Furthermore, permanent access to the victim of the abusive husband and the reduced ability of the women to defend herself make her appear an easy victim. What was surprising was that all eight women have given their inability to defend themselves the significance of cowardice, of weakness, of "stupidity", thus activating feelings of guilt and shame.

Data analysis and interpretation show that shame underlies women's behaviour of hiding, of avoiding personal failure that could be observed by someone, especially someone important to them. Breaking the silence and asking for help have the significance of a public exposure of their inability to raise at the standards of the "ideal I" meaning the risk of being condemned, judged and rejected. This is too much for the abused women.

The main danger at the base of the development of shame feeling is rejection or abandonment (Lewis, 1971) and has a double significance: the significance of well-deserved punishment for woman's failure to rise to internalized parental standards (*"I'm so ashamed in front of my parents"*) on one hand and the significance of the failure of the "ideal I" on the other hand. This double failure leads to the deep conviction that the women themselves are a failure.

Our conclusions support the results reported by the studies on adaptation, showing that seeking social support is avoided when the aim is to protect or increase self-esteem or social status (Folkman, Lazarus, Dunkel-Schetter, DeLongis & Gruen, 1986). Our data show that women experience recurrent feelings of shame that lead to the permanent interests in avoiding rejection and abandonment, *"a causal process which, in any case is likely to be an unconscious one. The identification of the experienced shame appears without the person necessarily aware of the family roots of the feeling, dating from early development, or its underlying motivations."* (Lazarus, 2011)

Suffering is even greater as fear, anxiety and guilt and tends to cause reactions of searching for help. The feeling of shame causes the woman victim to hide (Lazarus, 2011).

Addiction and Helplessness

The effects of domestic violence are devastating. What they all feel is the helplessness. Trapped in the "*hell of the marriage*" they don't have the power to escape. Despite suffering, most women find it difficult or even impossible to give up the initial commitment. This is what N. Gueguen identifies: "*...there are inside us some self-commitment processes which we hardly can break*" (Gueguen, 2007). To get out from this situation is almost impossible for the women, because they fear the violence directed against them or other family members or they don't have family or support and help in the community (Benninger-Budel & Lacroix 1999).

All forms of violence led finally to undermining of individual power. Life takes on the meaning of a solitary struggle for survival. All eight women made desperate efforts to keep the equilibrium within their environment; all they succeeded in doing was to perpetuate the violent environment in an altered form.

Helplessness is the loss of competence, which, in a generalization of the traumatic disillusion of oneself, may be described as disappointment. All eight life stories of the women included in this study reflect the fact that the traumatic situation is configured in a paradigm and also perceived as representative situation for the abused women. This leads to a change in the understanding of self and of the world that the woman had by then (Fischer & Riedesser, 2001).

If most people live with the illusory belief that death is far away, data analysis shows that the great majority of domestic violence victims are living close to death: "An experience of getting close to death will 'wake us from the illusion' in a way that we can designate as dysfunctional. It seems that we need a certain amount of illusion to master our lives" (Fischer & Riedesser, 2001). Losing illusions about major existential themes lead to the loss of hope and future prospects.

Conclusions

The domestic violence experience is one of torture. Trauma has to be understood not only today, but also from the life history of the abused woman.

In terms of information, traumatic situations lead the woman victim to process unbearable information, which exceeds her capacity to process.

Despite all the efforts of the women subjected to domestic violence, the experience of violence is unpredictable and impossible to anticipate; consequently, the "surprise" element returns along every act of violence. the categorization of information and the development of effective action plans become difficult. Psychological treatment of abused women need to consider the changes of those schemes developed after the experience of the domestic violence, with the aim of information processing and its integration.

Women as subjects of domestic violence seek to give significance to their experience of abuse; they need to make sense of these critical situations. This fact leads them to place the abuse experience in the larger context of survival. The only purpose is survival, any other explanation cannot be processed internally.

Experience of violence significantly lowers the sense of personal control, diluting to nothing any sense of self-worth, which has as its ultimate effect the inability to separate from the violent husband.

The experience of women subjected to domestic violence is built around the significance of "loss". Violence means for them the loss of illusions – those illusions "necessary to master our lives" (Fischer & Riedesser, 2001). They lost confidence in themselves and in others, in the safety of significant relationships, in the possibility to be helped. All these losses are accompanied by feelings of shame and guilt that are based on terrible fear of rejection and abandonment. Women victim behaviour is based on these meanings. Caught in the 'hell of their marriage', they lose hope and the ability to project themselves into a future without violence.

The complexities of domestic violence manifestations require complex intervention methods: from the governmental level to the social, medical, legal and psychological. Study results show that the experience of domestic violence is a traumatic one, which finally allows us to state that any psychological intervention on this issue should take into account following aspects:

-    Ensuring the security of women subjected to domestic violence and building a sense of security should be the basis for any work that is intended to be effective;

-    Establishing a relationship of trust, empathy and unconditional acceptance with the abused women;

-    Intervention must take into account the emotional relief and processing of trauma. Women must be helped to reconstruct self, and gain a sense of control and value over their lives.

Last but not least, we note that professionals in the field of domestic violence should receive special training in working with trauma.

References

Benninger-Budel, C. & Lacroix A. L. (1999). *Violence contre les femme. Raport OMCT.* Geneva: Eric Sottas, Directeur.

Brocki, J. M. & Wearden A. J. (2006). A critical evaluation of the use of interpretative phenomenological analysis (IPA) in health psychology. *Psychology & Health, 21*(1), 87–108.

Centrul de Resurse Juridice şi Institutul de Cercetare şi Prevenire a Criminalităţii. (2003). *Prevenirea şi intervenţia eficientă în violenţa domestic* [Effective prevention and intervention of domestic violence]. Bucureşti: Criminalităţii.

Centrul Parteneriat pentru Egalitate. (2003). *Cercetarea naţională privind violenţa în familie şi la locul de muncă* [National research on domestic violence and workplace]. Bucureşti: Criminalităţii.

Decision 686/2005 for approval of the National Strategy in the field of preventing and combating family violence. Published in the Official Monitor no. 367, May 29, 2003.

Fischer, G. Riedesser P. (2001). *Tratat de psichotraumatologie* [Tratat Psychological Trauma]. Bucureşti: Trei.

Folkman, S., Lazarus, R. S., Dunkel-Schetter C., DeLongis, A. Gruen, R. G. (1986). Dynamics of a stressful encounter: Cognitive appraisal, coping, and encounter outcomes. *Journal of Personality and Social Psychology, 50*(5), 992–1003.

Gueguen, N. (2007). *Psihologia supunerii si a manipularii* [The psychology of submission and handling]. Iasi: Polirom.

Killen, K. (2003). *Copilaria dureaza generatii la rand* [Childhood lasts for generations]. Timisoara: First,.

Larkin, M., Watts S. & Clifton, E. (2006). Giving voice and making sense in interpretative phenomenological analysis. *Qualitative Research in Psychology, 3*(2), 102–120.

Law 217/2003 on preventing and combating family violence. Published in the Official Monitor No. 678, May 25, 2005.

Lazarus, R. S. (2011). *Emotie si adaptare. O abordare cognitiva a proceselor afective* [Emotion and adaptation. A cognitive approach to affective processes]. Bucureşti: Trei.

Lewis, H. B. (1971). *Shame and guilt in neurosis* [Shame and guilt in neurosis]. New York: International Universities Press.

Muntean, A., Popescu, Marciana, Popa, Smaranda. (2000). *Victimele violentei domestice: copiii si femeile* [Victims of domestic violence: children and women]. Timisoara: Editura Eurostampa.

Muntean, A. & Munteanu A. (2011). *Violenta, Trauma, Rezilienta* [Violence, Trauma, Resilience]. Iasi: Polirom.

Mihaela Dana Bucută, Gabriela Dima

Riedesser, P. & Fischer G. (2007). *Tratat de psihotraumatologie. Fundamentele unui nou domeniu* [Psihotraumatologie treaty. Foundations of a new field]. Bucureşti: Editura Trei,.

Roth-Szamoskozi, M. (2005). *Copii si femei. Victime ale violentei* [Children and women. Victims of violence]. Cluj-Napoca: Presa Universitara Clujeana.

Smith, J. A. (1996). Beyond the divide between cognition and discourse: Using interpretative phenomenological analysis in health psychology. *Psychology & Health*, 11(2), 261–271.

Smith, J. A. (2004). Reflecting on the development of interpretative phenomenological analysis and its contribution to qualitative research in psychology. *Qualitative Research in Psychology*, *1*(1), 39–54.

Smith, J. & Osborn M. (2008). Interpretative Phenomenological Analysis. In J. Smith (Eds.), *Qualitative Psychology: A practical guide to research methods* (2nd ed.). London: Sage.

Stark, E. & Flitcraft A. (1996). *Women at Risk: Domestic Violence and Women's Health*. London: Sage Publications.

Walker, L. (1984). *The Battered Woman Syndrom*. New York: Springer.

Assessing psychodramatic intervention on female victims of violence. The cross-cultural validation of CORE-OM and SAI-R for Project Empower Daphne

Ines Testoni, Alessandra Armenti, Alice Bertoldo,
Daniela Di Lucia Sposito, Michael Wieser, Gabriela Moita,
Galabina Tarashoeva, Lucia Ronconi, Sibylla Verdi, Paolo Cottone

Introduction

This article presents the first part of the results obtained during project "EMPoWER" an action-research and longitudinal intervention that is part of the European Daphne III Program. The principal aim of this project is to intervene in the area of domestic violence perpetrated against women by utilizing both ecological counselling and psychodrama techniques, in order to study and modify the female victimization process. In fact, the intervention has helped women to become aware of the history of their condition and to change the unconscious dynamics which perpetuate their subjugation, so as to achieve resiliency and improve effective self-determination. Theoretically, Empower belongs to the field of gender studies on "female agency", which has played an important role in denoting the intellectual capacity of women to make intelligent, purposeful and rational decisions, despite social influences and control, and the action of pervasive systems in which men dominate, oppress and exploit women (DesAutels & Urban Walker, 2004). Through the active psychodramatic methods employed, which involve the reconstruction of their role of victim, the women can understand how their condition is the result of their cultural situation. In this article, we discuss the results inherent to the construction of parameters and the validation devised to assess the efficacy of both ecological counselling and psychodramatic intervention.

As per the Morenian psychodramatic perspective (1947), the first key-construct of project Empower is "spontaneity", which is considered as the main psychological tool for promoting agency and resilience leading to behavioural change. Similar to the more recent studies on gender which discuss the female process of emancipation from subordination to the acquisition of "agency" power, i.e. the conscious ability to modify crystallized scripts and to change behaviour for personal empowerment (McNay, 2000), Moreno (1947) indicated earlier that spontaneity is the condition that a person must achieve in order to feel an emotion and become aware of it and thus play a role voluntarily. Furthermore, Moreno (1947) emphasized the close connection between spontaneity and psychological well-being: the more a person is spontaneous the more they are well. We agree with Moreno and Maslow (1970) who consider the ability to be spontaneous as a prerequisite for the achievement of self-realization and mental health. In addition, Steitzel and Hughey (1994) confirmed that spontaneity is a necessary prerequisite to experiencing joy and deep satisfaction. Unfortunately, for a long time the only available measure of spontaneity remained scientifically inaccurate, until finally, in 2005, Kipper and Hundal completed the Spontaneity Assessment Inventory-revised (SAI-R), a questionnaire initially devised by Moreno for the assessment of spontaneity. The studies carried out by Kipper and Shemer (2006) have shown that the original SAI, was positively correlated with various dimensions that have to do with well-being. The SAI-R poses one initial question: *"How strongly do you have these feelings and thoughts during a typical day?"*. The question is followed by a list consisting of 18 items, some are adjectives and others are phrases that describe different feelings and thoughts. The participants respond by expressing an opinion on a five-point Likert scale.

The second main construct of the Empower project was "well-being". According to the Fepto Research Program[1], this construct can be assessed by the CORE (Evans et al. 2002), which was administered in order to check the effectiveness of the Empower interventions (Testoni et al. 2012; 2013). It is composed of three interdependent instruments. The first is the CORE-OM (Outcome Measure), which is a 34 item patient questionnaire (5-point Likert scale, based on how frequently they experienced a certain mood during the last week). The CORE instrument is also made-up of other sections like the CORE-A (Assessment), which is a form that has to be filled out by the therapist. We did not use this tool. The form gathers anagraphical and personal information in relation to how the individual felt prior to therapy, on the severity (Likert 4 point scale) and on the duration of the disorder (<6 months, 6-12 months, >12 months, re-occurring-continuous). There is also an End of Therapy Form, which is a form filled out by the therapist that describes the progress of therapy and details the end of therapy procedure, together with a series of subjective evaluations on the treatment outcome. In the present study, we will use the CORE-OM to investigate the construct of psychologi-

---

1   FEPTO, http://www.fepto.eu/

cal well-being. The items on the CORE-OM relate to four specific domains: Subjective well-being; Symptoms/Problems; Functioning and Risk.

The third main construct of Empower project was "depression", investigated through Beck Depression Inventory – II (BDI-II). The BDI-II is a self evaluation tool that measures the severity of depression developed around the assessment of symptoms corresponding to diagnostic criteria of depressive symptoms listed in the Diagnostic and Statistical Manual of Mental Disorder – Fourth Edition (DSM-IV; American Psychiatric Association, 1994). The original version of the BDI, developed by Aaron T. Beck and associates in 1961, consists of a group of 21 items corresponding to the main symptoms most commonly reported by depressed psychiatric patients, but not by non-depressed psychiatric patients, without any particular reference to a specific theoretical approach to depression (Beck et al. 1961).

The BDI-II is made up of 21 groups of statements about symptoms and depressive moods. For each group of statements, the subject is asked to respond by choosing the statement that best describes how they have felt "in the last two weeks (including today)"; each group of statements is followed by four possible options, from a scale of 0 to 4, indicating how much that symptom or attitude has increased or decreased over the past two weeks, where the value of zero indicates that there has been no change. The present study aims to review the cross-cultural relationship between the construct of spontaneity and psychological well-being and depression in six different European countries and to observe the relationship between gender, spontaneity, psychological well-being and depression.

Hypothesis

The purpose of this report is to verify our theoretical model, enable us to set the underlying assumptions for the six countries studied (Italy, Austria, Portugal, Romania, Bulgaria and Albania), and make cross-cultural comparisons including comparing gender-culture score differences to verify the importance of spontaneity and provide significant validation of the measures and model.

Spontaneity also acts on personal well-being through its close relationship with the intrinsic motivation of the person and their internal voluntary drive to reach a goal. Moreover, high levels of spontaneity are related to a sense of personal self-efficacy, whereas low levels of spontaneity lead to low self-esteem, depression and thoughts of a negative and denigrating nature towards oneself and external situations.

Method
Participants and measures

A total of 814 University students participated in the study (see Table 1); 407 females and 407 males, aged between 18 and 24 years ($M = 20,58$ years; $SD = 1,48$), in six European Countries: Italy, Austria, Bulgaria, Portugal, Romania and Albania.

All individuals took part voluntarily and with no payment for participation.

| Country | N | Gender | | Age (years) | | |
		Female	Male	Range	M	SD
Italy	166	83	83	19-24	20.99	1.38
Austria	146	73	73	18-24	20.68	1.38
Bulgaria	126	63	63	18-24	19.88	1.73
Portugal	134	67	67	18-24	20.73	1.61
Romania	104	53	52	18-24	20.44	1.16
Albania	138	69	69	18-24	20.57	1.27
Total	814	407	407	18-24	20.58	1.48

Table.1 European Samples

Bulgarian, Portuguese, Romanian and Albanian participants were administered the two main instruments individually and anonymously: SAI-R Spontaneity Assessment Inventory-Revised (Kipper & Shemer, 2006) and CORE-OM Clinical Outcomes for Routine Evaluation-Outcome Measure (Evans et al. 2002). For the Italian and Austrian participants we administered one more instrument to measure depression: the BDI-II Beck Depression Inventory-II version (Beck et al. 1996). The questionnaire included a socio-demographic form (age, gender, marital status, children, occupation and education) together with the two assessment tools for Bulgaria, Portugal, Romania and Albania, along with three assessment tools for Italy and Austria (Testoni et al. 2013; 2012).

Results
SAI-R

The literature reports that the Cronbach's alpha reliability coefficient of the SAI-R is .79 (Kipper et al. 2005; 2006; 2009). The average score on the SAI-R was *66.41, SD = 10.16*, and no significant differences for either gender were found.

ITALIAN SAMPLE. For the Italian sample, Cronbach's Alpha for the SAI-R was .81 (95% CI .76 to .85). The average score on the SAI-R was 57.05 (*SD* = 8.09), which corresponds to a good level of spontaneity according to the criteria for a non clinical sample, such as the sample investigated. Contrary to that reported in the literature, in the Italian sample there were statistically significant differences between the scores obtained by females (*M* = 55.38, *SD* = 7.58) and males (*M* = 58.71, *SD* = 8.28) on the SAI-R, $t(164) = -2.70$, $p < .01$; in fact, we reported significantly higher scores for men.

AUSTRIAN SAMPLE. For the Austrian sample, Cronbach's Alpha for the SAI-R was .91. The average on the total score was 63.70 (*SD* = 9.83), which corresponds to a good level of spontaneity.

BULGARIAN SAMPLE. For the Bulgarian sample, Cronbach's Alpha for the SAI-R was .86. The average score on the SAI-R was 60.17 (*SD* = 11.35), which corresponds to a good level of spontaneity according to the criteria for a non clinical sample, such as the sample investigated.

PORTUGUESE SAMPLE. For the Portuguese sample, Cronbach's Alpha for the SAI-R was .89. The average score on the SAI-R was 64.44 (*SD* = 8.13), which corresponds to a good level of spontaneity according to the criteria for a non clinical sample, such as the sample investigated. Contrary to that reported in the literature, in the Portuguese sample there were statistically significant differences between the scores obtained by females (*M* = 62.93, *SD* = 7.42) and males (*M* = 65.96, *SD* = 8.58) on the SAI-R, $t(132) = -2.19$, $p < .05$; in fact, we reported significantly higher scores for men.

ROMANIAN SAMPLE. For the Romanian sample, Cronbach's Apha for the SAI-R was .93. The average score on the SAI-R was 61.34 (*SD* = 12.28), which corresponds to a good level of spontaneity according to the criteria for a non clinical sample, such as the sample investigated.

ALBANIAN SAMPLE. For the Albanian sample, Cronbach's Apha for the SAI-R was .88. The average score on the SAI-R was 62.46 (*SD* = 11.06), which corresponds to a good level of spontaneity according to the criteria for a non clinical sample, such as the sample investigated. Contrary to that reported in the literature, in the Albanian sample there were statistically significant differences between the scores obtained by females (*M* = 59.93, *SD* = 9.29) and males (*M* = 65.00, *SD* = 12.14) on the SAI-R, $t(136) = -2.75$, $p < .01$; in fact, we reported significantly higher scores for men.

CORE-OM

In the literature, the internal consistency of the CORE-OM is .94 (.93 to .95) and for each of the domains the Alpha values were: Well-being (W) α = .77 (.75 to .79), Problems (P) α = .90 (.89 to .91), Functioning (F) α = .86 (.85 to .87), Risk (R) α = .79 (.77 to .81), Non-risk items (-R) α = .94 (.93 to .95). The average score was .76 (*SD* = .59), and for each of the CORE-OM domains: Well-being (W) *M* =.91 (*SD* = .83), Problems (P) *M* = .90 (*SD* =.72), Functioning (F) *M* = .85 (*SD* = .65), Risk (R) *M* = .20 (*SD* = .45) and Non-risk items (-R) *M* = .88 (*SD* = .66). No significant differences for either gender were found.

ITALIAN SAMPLE. For the Italian sample, Cronbach's Alpha for the CORE-OM was .90 (95% CI .87 to .92). The average of the total score of the CORE-OM was .99 (*SD* = .45) and this corresponds to a good level of psychological well-being according to the criteria for a non-clinical sample, like the sample investigated. The averages for the specific domains were the following: Well-being (W) *M* = 1.27 (*SD* = .74); Problems (P) *M* = 1.15 (*SD* = .63); Functioning (F) *M* = 1.13 (*SD* = .48); Risk (R) *M* = 1.17 (*SD* = .33) and Non-risk items (-R) *M* = .85 (*SD* = .52). Contrary to that reported in the literature, in the Italian sample there were statistically significant differences between the scores obtained by females (*M* = 1.12, *SD* = .49) and males (*M* = .85, *SD* = .36) on the CORE-OM, *t*(164) = 3.97, *p* <.001; in fact, we reported significantly higher scores for women.

AUSTRIAN SAMPLE. For the Austrian sample, Cronbach's Alpha for the CORE-OM was .92 (95% CI .90 to .94), a value very similar to that reported in studies by Evans et al. (2002) The average of the total scores of the CORE-OM was .74 (*SD* = .49) and corresponds to a good level of psychological well-being according to criteria for non-clinical samples. The averages of the specific domains were: Well-being (W) *M* = .82 (*SD* = .68); Problems (P) *M* = .94 (*SD* = .71); Functioning (F) *M* = .85 (*SD* = .52); Risk (R) *M* = .10 (*SD* = .25) and Non-risk items (-R) *M* = .88 (*SD* = .57).

BULGARIAN SAMPLE. For the Bulgarian sample, Cronbach's Alpha for the CORE-OM was .85. The average of the total scores of the CORE-OM was 1.40 (*SD* =.43). The averages of the specific domains were: Well-being (W) *M* = 2.03 (*SD* = .54); Problems (P) *M* = 1.24 (*SD* =.75); Functioning (F) *M* = 1.93 (*SD* = .40); Risk (R) *M* = .21 (*SD* = .49) and Non-risk items (-R) *M* = .1.65 (*SD* = .46).

PORTUGUESE SAMPLE. For the Portuguese sample, Cronbach's Alpha for the CORE-OM was .85. The average of the total scores of the CORE-OM was 1.36 (*SD* = .37). The averages of the specific domains were: Well-being (W) *M* = 1.87 (*SD* = .42); Problems (P) *M* = 1.21 (*SD* =.69); Functioning (F) *M* = 1.89 (*SD* = .31); Risk (R) *M* = .28 (*SD* = .39) and Non-risk items (-R) *M* = .1.59 (*SD* = .41).

ROMANIAN SAMPLE. For the Romanian sample, Cronbach's Alpha for the CORE-OM was .85.The average of the total scores on the CORE-OM was 1.36 (SD =.43). The averages of the specific domains were: Well-being (W) M = 1.87 (SD = .57); Problems (P) M = 1.29 (SD =.77); Functioning (F) M = 1.79 (SD = .39); Risk (R) M = .31 (SD = .50) and Non-risk items (-R) M = .1.58 (SD = .46). Contrary to that reported in the literature, in the Romanian sample there were statistically significant differences between the scores obtained by females (M = 1.44, SD = .46) and males (M = 1.28, SD =.38) on the CORE-OM, $t(102)$ = 2.04, p < .05; in fact, we reported significantly higher scores for women.

ALBANIAN SAMPLE. For the Albanian sample, Cronbach's Alpha for the CORE-OM was .91, a value very similar to that reported in studies by Evans et al. (2002) The average of the total scores of the CORE-OM was 1.05 (SD =.53). The averages of the specific domains were: Well-being (W) M = 1.35 (SD = .91); Problems (P) M = 1.26 (SD =.70); Functioning (F) M = 1.14 (SD = .52); Risk (R) M = .24 (SD = .43) and Non-risk items (-R) M = 1.22 (SD = .59).

BDI-II

In the literature, the internal consistency of the BDI-II is. 91, the average score on the SAI-R was *8.20, SD* = *5.60*, and significant differences for gender were found, in fact, we reported significantly higher scores for women.

ITALIAN SAMPLE. For the Italian sample, Cronbach's Alpha for the BDI-II was .87 (95% CI .83 to .89).The average score on the BDI-II was 8.59 (SD = 6.69), which corresponds to a low level of depression according to the criteria for a non clinical sample, such as the sample investigated. As reported in the literature, in the Italian sample there were statistically significant differences between the scores obtained by females (M = 10.69, SD = 8.24) and males (M =6.49, SD = 3.63) on the BDI-II, $t(164)$ = 4.25, p <.001; in fact, we reported significantly higher scores for women.

AUSTRIAN SAMPLE. For the Austrian sample, Cronbach's Alpha for the BDI-II was .81 (95% CI .76 to .85). The average of the total score was 5.96 (SD = 4.97), which corresponds to a low level of depression according to the criteria for a non clinical sample. Contrary to that reported in the literature, in the Austrian sample there were no statistically significant differences between the scores obtained by females and males.

Contrary to that reported in the literature, in the Italian sample there were statistically significant differences between the scores obtained by females (M = 10.69, SD = 8.24) and males (M = 6.49, SD = 3.63) on the BDI-II, $t(166)$ = -2.70, p < .01; in fact, we reported significantly higher scores for women.

Correlations between scores

The following section presents the results of the correlations between the instruments for each country in order to verify if the pattern of negative correlations between SAI-R, CORE-OM and BDI-II is confirmed in each country considered in the study and the total sample. Then we will present the overall comparisons between Italy, Bulgaria, Portugal, Albania, Romania and Austria and compare that to the average total scores obtained in the test in addition to considering gender differences in the various countries.

	M	SD	CORE-OM	W	P	F	R	-R	SAI-R	BDI-II
CORE-OM	.99	.45	-	.81**	.92**	.87**	.42**	.99**	-.47**	.74**
W	1.27	.74		.	.74**	.62**	.16*	.83**	-.50**	.64**
P	1.15	.63			.	.66**	.27**	.93**	-.39**	.71**
F	1.13	.48				.	.34**	.87**	-.46**	.62**
R	.17	.33					.	.31**	-.01*	.26**
-R	1.16	.52						.	-.49**	.74**
SAI-R	57.05	8.09							.	-.33**
BDI-II	8.59	6.69								.

Note:* $p < .05$, ** $p < .01$

Table 2. Correlations CORE-OM, SAI-R and BDI-II, Italian sample($N= 166$)

Table 2 shows the correlations between SAI-R, CORE-OM and BDI-II in the Italian sample. There was a negative correlation between the instruments ($r = -.47, p < .001$; $r = -.33, p < .001$). We also observed negative correlations for CORE-OM specific domains with SAI-R and BDI-II (W, $r = -.50, p < .001$; P, $r = -.39, p < .001$; F, $r = -.46, p < .001$; R, $r = -.01, p < .001$; -R, $r = -.49, p < .001$).

Table 3 highlights the correlations between SAI-R, CORE-OM and BDI-II in the Austrian sample. Our results confirm the negative correlations between the instruments ($r = -.54, p < .001$; $r = -.58, p < .001$). We also observed negative correlations for CORE-OM specific domains with SAI-R and BDI-II (W, $r = -.51, p < .001$; P, $r = -.48, p < .001$; F, $r = -.51, p < .001$; R, $r = -.18, p < .001$; -R, $r = -.54, p < .001$).

	M	SD	CORE-OM	W	P	F	R	-R	SAI-R	BDI-II
CORE-OM	.74	.49	-	.87**	.94**	.91**	.47**	.99**	4**	.66**
W	.82	.68		.	.77**	.78**	.31**	.88**	1**	.55**
P	.94	.71			.	.72**	.36**	.94**	3**	.64**
F	.85	.52				.	.41**	.90**	1**	.56**
R	.10	.25					.	.40**	-.18*	.36**
-R	.88	.57						.	4**	.65**
SAI-R	63.70	9.84							.	-.58**
BDI-II	5.96	4.97								.

Note:* $p < .05$, ** $p < .01$

Table 3. Correlations CORE-OM, SAI-R and BDI-II, Austrian sample ($N= 146$)

	M	SD	CORE-OM	W	P	F	R	-R	SAI-R
CORE-OM	1.40	.43	-	.55**	.89**	.72**	.63**	.98**	-.36**
W	2.03	.54		-	.33**	.48**	.15**	.58**	-.08*
P	1.24	.75			-	.39**	.45**	.90**	-.40**
F	1.93	.40				-	.39**	.73**	-.14**
R	.21	.49					-	.50**	-.29**
-R	1.65	.46						-	-.34**
SAI-R	60.17	11.35							-

Note:* $p < .05$, ** $p < .01$

Table 4. Correlations: CORE-OM and SAI-R, Bulgarian sample ($N = 126$)

In Table 4 the correlations between SAI-R and CORE-OM for the Bulgarian sample are reported. In Bulgaria we found a negative correlation between the instruments ($r = -.363$, $p < .001$). We also observed negative correlations for CORE-OM on specific domains with SAI-R (W, $r = -.08$, $p < .001$; P, $r = -.40$, $p < .001$; F, $r = -.14$, $p < .001$; R, $r = -.29$, $p < .001$; -R, $r = -.34$, $p < .001$).

	M	SD	CORE-OM	W	P	F	R	-R	SAI-R
CORE-OM	1.36	.37	-	.60**	.93**	.68**	.64**	.99**	-.37**
W	1.87	.42		-	.42**	.49**	.26**	.62**	-.14**
P	1.21	.69			-	.42**	.52**	.93**	-.44**
F	1.89	.31				-	.28**	.71**	-.07**
R	.28	.39					-	.51**	-.24**
-R	1.59	.41						-	-.37**
SAI-R	64.44	8.13							-

Note:* p < .05, ** p < .01

Table 5. Correlations: CORE-OM and SAI-R, Portuguese sample (N= 134)

Table 5 illustrates the correlations between SAI-R and CORE-OM in the Portuguese sample. In Portugal we found a negative correlation between the instruments ($r = -.37, p < .001$). We also observed negative correlations on CORE-OM specific domains with SAI-R (W, $r = -.14, p < .001$; P, $r = -.44$, $p < .001$; F, $r = -.07, p < .001$; R, $r = -.24, p < .001$; -R, $r = -.37, p < .001$).

	M	SD	CORE-OM	W	P	F	R	-R	SAI-R
CORE-OM	1.36	.43	-	.50**	.91**	.68**	.62**	.98**	-.56**
W	1.87	.57		-	.27**	.49**	.06**	.55**	-.03**
P	1.29	.77			-	.38**	.53**	.90**	-.66**
F	1.79	.39				-	.19**	.72**	-.17**
R	.31	.50					-	.46**	-.35**
-R	1.58	.46						-	-.54**
SAI-R	61.34	12.28							-

Note:* p < .05, ** p < .01

Table 6. Correlations: CORE-OM and SAI-R, Romanian sample (N= 104)

Table 6 shows the correlations between SAI-R and CORE-OM in the Romanian sample. In Romania we found a negative correlation between the instruments ($r = -.56, p < .001$). We also observed negative correlations for CORE-OM specific domains with SAI-R (W, $r = -.03, p < .001$; P, $r = -.66$, $p < .001$; F, $r = -.17, p < .001$; R, $r = -.35, p < .001$; -R, $r = -.54, p < .001$).

	M	SD	CORE-OM	W	P	F	R	-R	SAI-R
CORE-OM	1.05	.53	-	.84**	.93**	.88**	.61**	.99**	-.69**
W	1.35	.91		-	.78**	.64**	.35**	.86**	-.58**
P	1.26	.70			-	.70**	.43**	.95**	-.59**
F	1.14	.52				-	.55**	.88**	-.69**
R	.24	.43					-	.50**	-.41**
-R	1.22	.59						-	-.69**
SAI-R	62.46	11.06							-

Note:* p < .05, ** p < .01

Table 7. Correlations: CORE-OM and SAI-R, Albanian sample ($N= 138$)

Table 7 illustrates the correlations between SAI-R and CORE-OM in the Albanian sample. There was a negative correlation between the instruments (r = -.69, p < .001). We also observed negative correlations on CORE-OM specific domains with SAI-R (W, r = -.58, p < .001; P, r = -.59, p < .001; F, r = -.69, p < .001; R, r = -.41, p < .001; -R, r = -.69, p < .001).

	M	SD	CORE-OM	W	P	F	R	-R	SAI-R
CORE-OM	1.13	.51	-	.81**	.86**	.84**	.54**	.99**	-.43**
W	1.50	.79		-	.56**	.74**	.25**	.83**	-.29**
P	1.17	.71			-	.48**	.44**	.86**	-.48**
F	1.41	.62				-	.34**	.86**	-.26**
R	.21	.40					-	.44**	-.25**
-R	1.32	.58						-	-.43**
SAI-R	61.41	10.38							-

Note:* p < .05, ** p < .01

Table 8. Correlations: SAI-R and CORE-OM, total sample (N = 814)

Table 8 illustrates the correlations between SAI-R and CORE-OM in the total sample. The total sample reported a negative correlation between the instruments (r = -.43, p< .001). We also observed negative correlations for the CORE-OM specific domains with SAI-R (W, r = -.29, p < .001; P, r = -.48, p < .001; F, r = -.26, p < .001; R, r = -.25, p< .001; -R, r = -.43, p < .001).

In Summary, in each Country the results confirm the hypothesis that there is an inverse relationship between indices of spontaneity and psychological well-being. Also in the total sample there is a negative correlation between the instruments that establishes the inverse relationship between spontaneity and psychopathology and depression.

Comparisons between Countries
SAI-R

Anova 2x6 on SAI-R scores (see Table 9) shows significant differences between Countries [$F(5, 812) = 11.03; p < .001$)], significant gender differences [$F(1,802) = 7.21; p < .01$] and a significant relationship gender x country [$F(5,802) = 2.65; p < .05$].

	Male		Female	
Country				
	M	SD	M	SD
Italy	58.71	8.28	55.38	7.58
Austria	63.48	9.58	63.92	10.14
Bulgaria	65.96	8.58	62.93	7.42
Portugal	58.90	11.90	61.44	10.71
Romania	62.81	13.19	59.87	11.24
Albania	65.00	12.14	59.93	9.29
Total	62.38	10.88	60.44	9.76

Table 9. Descriptive statistics (Gender x Country), SAI-R

Main effect Country. For the Italian sample, the post-hoc analysis with the Bonferroni method showed significantly lower average t test scores compared to other Countries, but not for Bulgaria (Portugal, $d = -7.39$ $p < .001$; Austria, $d = -6.65$ $p < .001$; Albania, $d = -5.41$ $p < .001$; Romania, $d = -4.29$ $p < .01$ and Bulgaria $d = -3.13$ p = .123). The Portuguese sample scored significantly higher on tests compared to the Bulgarian sample ($d = 4.27$ p < .01).

Main effect Gender. The results show that males have a higher mean score than females on the test ($d = .90$ p < .01).

Interaction Country x Gender. Consistent with the findings in the literature (Christoforou & Kipper, 2006), no significant differences for gender in the Austrian, Portuguese, Bulgarian and Romanian samples were found on the SAI-R. In contrast to the study of Kipper & Shemer (2006), we observed statistically significant gender differences in the Italian and Albanian samples.

The post-hoc analysis using the Bonferroni method showed gender differences only in Italy ($d = 3.33$ p < .05) and in Albania ($d = 5.07$ p < .01). Figure 1 provides a notched boxplot of all data.

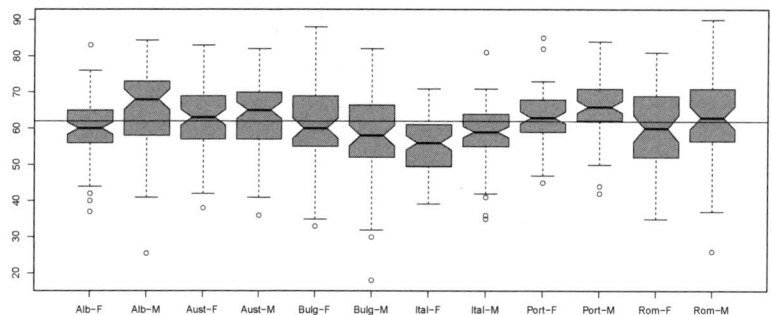

Figure 1. SAI-R by Gender and Country

CORE-OM

Anova 2x6 on CORE-OM scores (see Table 10) showed significant differences between countries [$F_{(5, 812)} = 11.03$; p < .001)], significant gender differences [$F_{(1,802)} = 6.17$ p < .05] and a significant relationship gender x country [$F_{(5,802)} = 2.53$ p < .05].

Country	Male		Female	
	M	SD	M	SD
Italy	.85	.36	1.12	.49
Austria	.73	.47	.76	.51
Bulgaria	1.43	.50	1.36	.34
Portugal	1.34	.33	1.39	.41
Romania	1.28	.38	1.44	.46
Albania	1.03	.51	1.06	.55
Total	1.08	.50	1.17	.52

Table 10. Descriptive statistics (Gender x Country), CORE-OM

Main effect Country. In Austria, a post-hoc analysis using the Bonferroni method showed significantly lower average test scores compared to other Countries (Bulgaria d = -.65 p < .001; Portugal and Romania d = -.62 p < .001; Albania d =-.30 p < .001; Italy d = -.24 p < .001). Italy reported a lower average test score compared to Bulgaria (d = -.41; p < .001), Portugal (d =-.38; p < .001) and Romania (d = -.37; p < .001). The average score in the Albanian sample was significantly lower compared to the Bulgarian (d = -.35 p < .001), Portuguese and Romanian sample (d = -.31 p < .001).

Main effect Gender. The male sample reported a lower mean score than the females (d = -.08 p < .05).

Interaction Country x Gender Contrary to what is reported in the literature, in the Italian sample there were statistically significant differences between the scores obtained by females and males on the CORE-OM. The post-hoc analysis with the Bonferroni method revealed significant gender differences only in Italy (d = -.27 p < .001). Figure 2 gives a notched boxplot of all data.

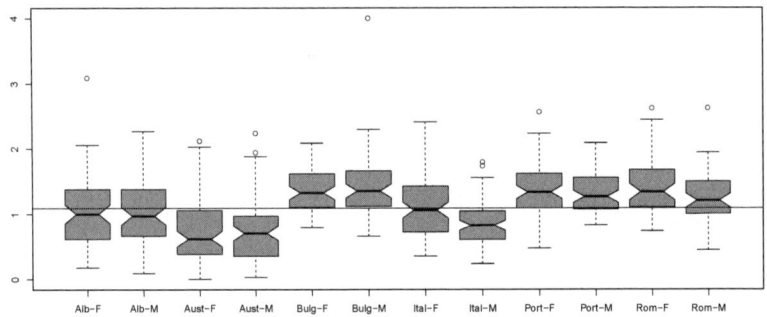

Figure 2. CORE-OM by Gender and Country

BDI-II

An Anova 2x6 on BDI-II test scores (see Table 11) showed significant differences between Countries [$F(1, 308)$ = 16.16; p < .001)], significant gender differences [$F(1,308)$ = 7.78 p < .01] and a significant relationship gender x country [$F(1,308)$ = 13.21 p < .001].

Country	Male		Female	
	M	SD	M	SD
Italy	6.49	3.63	10.69	8.25
Austria	6.24	4.86	5.69	5.10
Total	6.37	4.24	8.35	7.37

Table 11. Descriptive statistics (Gender x Country), BDI-II

Main effect Country. The results showed significantly lower average test scores in Austria compared to the other Countries (d = -2.63 p < .001).

Main effect Gender. The results report that males had a mean score on the test, lower than females (d = -1.82 p < .01).

Interaction Country x Gender Consistent with the findings in the literature (Beck et al. 1996), significant differences for gender in the Italian samples were founder for the BDI-II. A Post-hoc analysis with the Bonferroni method showed gender differences only in Italy (d = -4.20 p < .001), where women score significantly higher. Figure 3 provides a notched boxplot of all data.

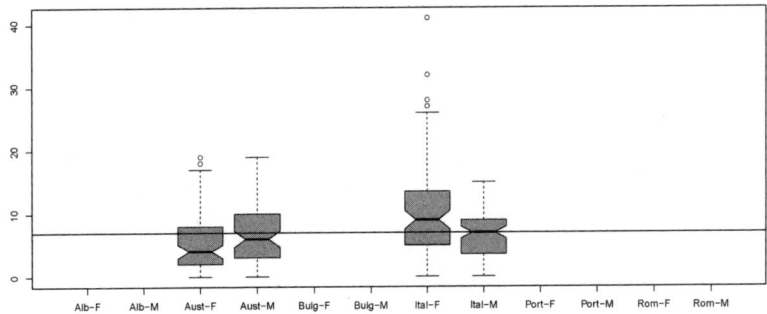

Figure 3. BDI-II by Gender and Country

Discussion

The objective of this study was to verify the validity of the assessment of project Empower, based on the administration of two instruments (SAI-R and CORE-OM) and to report on the change in the psychological condition of women that have been victims of domestic violence. The women involved in the project, were tested after ecological counselling and psychodramatic intervention conducted in various antiviolence centres in Austria, Albania,

Bulgaria, Italy, Portugal and Romania. Since victims of violence can develop depressive traits, in order to consider the correlation between the constructs of spontaneity (measured by SAI-R) and well-being (CORE-OM), we also measured the correlation between them and the BDI-II, in Austria and Italy. It was not possible to administer the BDI-II in all of the Countries involved in the project because the instrument has not been validated in all countries. The analysis of the correlation between the three instruments in Austria and Italy has already been discussed in detail in Testoni et al. (2013), therefore we will just briefly touch on the main results. The data from the analysis of the individual instruments in the two countries reported very high values of internal consistency in all cases; the three instruments are correlated and in particular: SAI-R is correlated negatively and the CORE-OM is correlated positively with BDI-II. These results allow us to infer hypothetically that the SAI-R and CORE-OM assessment in addition to measuring spontaneity and well-being, may indicate the continuity of latent depressive traits in victims.

The results of this initial phase enables us to claim that the instrument SAI-R/CORE-OM may be considered valid for detecting possible changes in T1/T2 with respect to the women participating in the Empower project. In fact, in every country we confirmed our hypothesized correlation. In particular in Italy and Austria, we detected a positive correlation between the CORE-OM and the BDI-II, in all the countries we detected a negative correlation between the SAI-R/CORE-OM and in Italy and Austria there was a negative correlation between the BDI-II and the SAI-R.

With regard to *Gender Effects*, we note that, contrary to what is reported in the literature, there was a significant difference on the SAI-R scores (Kipper et al. 2006), which is greater in males than in females. In Italy and Austria, there was also a significant gender difference on the BDI-II, already reported in the literature (Beck et al. 1996), that is greater in females than in males. Contrary to what is reported in the literature (Evans et al. 2002), there was a significant gender difference on the CORE-OM, that is greater in females than in males.

In relation to *Country Effect*, Italy had lower SAI-R test scores compared to all the other countries except Bulgaria and the latter is characterized by lower scores than those recorded in Portugal. Austria had CORE-OM scores that were lower compared to all the other countries; Italy and Albania had scores that were lower than Bulgaria, Portugal and Romania.

Austria had lower scores than Italy on the BDI-II. In the final assessment concerning the effect of counselling and psychodrama intervention, we shall take into account the relationship between country effect and the specific results at T1-T2 of the women participating in the project.

References

Beck, Aaron T., Robert A. Steer and Gregory K. Brown (1996). *Manual for the Beck Depression Inventory — (BDI-II)*, 2nd ed. San Antonio, TX: Psychological Corporation.

Christoforou, Androulla and David A. Kipper (2006). *The Spontaneity Assessment Inventory (SAI), Anxiety, obsessive-compulsive tendency, and temporal orientation*. Philadelphia, PA: Heldref Publications.

DesAutels, Peggy and Margaret Urban Walker (2004). *Moral Psychology: Feminist Ethics and Social Theory*. New York: Rowman and Littlefield.

Evans Chris, Janice Connell, Michael Barkham, Frank Margison, Graeme McGrath, John Mellor-Clark and Kerry Audin (2002). "Towards a standardised brief outcome measure: Psychometric properties and utility of the CORE-OM." *British Journal of Psychiatry* 180: 51–60.

FEPTO. "Research – Photo archive." http://www.fepto.eu/web/en/ Organisation/ Research_-_Photo_archive/ (accessed December 11, 2012)

FEPTO. http://www.fepto.eu/web/en/Organisation/Committees_/ (accessed November 13, 2011).

Kipper, David A. and Haim Shemer (2006). "The Spontaneity Assessment Inventory-Revised (SAI-R): Spontaneity, well-being and stress." *Journal of Group Psychotherapy, Psychodrama & Sociometry* 59, no. 3: 127–136.

Kipper, David A. and Jasdeep Hundal (2005). "The Spontaneity Assessment Inventory: the Relationship between spontaneity and Nonspontaneity." *Journal of Group Psychotherapy, Psychodrama & Sociometry* 58, no. 3: 119–129.

Kipper, David. A. and Eva Buras (2009). "Measurement of spontaneity: The relationship between the intensity and frequency of the spontaneous experience." *Perceptual and Motor Skills* 108, no. 2: 362–366.

Maslow, Abraham H. (1970). *Motivation and personality*, 2nd ed. New York: Harper & Row.

McNay, Lois (2000). *Gender and agency: Reconfiguring the subject in feminist and social theory*. Cambridge: Polity.

Moreno, Jacob L. (1947). *The theatre of spontaneity*. New York: Beacon House.

Stietzel, Lynne D. and Andrew R. Hughey. *Empowerment through spontaneity: A taste of psychodrama*. San Jose, CA: Associates for Community Interaction Press, 1994.

Testoni I, Armenti, A., Ronconi, L., Wieser, M., Zamperini, A., Verdi, S., Evans, C. (2013). *Violência de gênero. Testando um modelo: espontaneidade, bem-estar psicológico e depressão*. [Gender Violence. Testing a model of assumptions: spontaneity, psychological well-being and depression]. Rev Bras Psicodrama [Brazilian Journal of Psychodrama], 21(1), in press.

Testoni, I., Armenti, A., Guglielmin, M.S., Ronconi, L., Zamperini, A., Cottone, P., Wieser, M., Dima, G., Moita, G., Terashoeva, G., Bucuta, M. (2012). *Em-*

power: A Daphne III project- the mission, the structure and the results. Interdisciplinary Journal of Family Studies, XVII, 2/2012.

Testoni, I., Armenti, A., Guglielmin, M.S., Ronconi, L., Zamperini, A., Cottone, P., Wieser, M., Dima, G., Moita, G., Terashoeva, G., Bucuta, M. *The efficaciousness of Empower project: Psychodrama and elaboration of family violence.* ATGENDER – vol. 2. Teaching against violence. Reassessing the toolbox, in press.

Testoni,I., Armenti, A., Ronconi, L., Cottone, P., Wieser, M., Verdi, S. (2012). *Daphne European Research Project: Italian Validation of Hypothesis Model (SAI-R, CORE-OM and BDI-II)* Interdisciplinary Journal of Family Studies, XVII, 1/2012.

Authors

Caterina Arcidiacono: Professor of Community Psychology Coordinator of the PhD Doctoral School in Psychology, Pedagogy and Linguistic Coordinator of the Phd Doctoral Course in Gender Studies Federico II University, Naples e-mail: caterina.arcidiacono@unina.it

Alessandra Armenti: PhD, Post-doctoral researcher IClab "Interaction & Culture Lab", Department of Philosophy, Sociology, Education & Applied Psychology (FISPPA), University of Padua (Italy), email: alessandra.armenti@unipd.it

Gill Bell: Psychologist and professor at Gerda Boyesen International Institute of Biodynamic Psychology and Psychotherapy, London and Killala, Co Mayo, Ireland, email: gillbell@biodynamic.org

Alice Bertoldo: Research & Editorial Research Associate Gender and Women Studies (focus on VAW) for EMPoWER – Daphne III, Department of Philosophy, Sociology, Education & Applied Psychology (FISPPA), Section of Applied Psychology, University of Padua (Italy) email: alice.bertoldo@unipd.it

Paolo Cottone: Researcher and director of Clab "Interaction & Culture Lab" at Department of Philosophy, Sociology, Education & Applied Psychology (FISPPA), Section of Applied Psychology University of Padova, email: paolo.cottone@unipd.it

Mihaela Dana Bucuță: Romanian Association of Classical Psychodrama. "Lucian Blaga", Associate lecturer at University of Sibiu, Romania, email: bucutamihaela@yahoo.com

Daniela Di Lucia Sposito: Research & Editorial Research Associate Gender and Women Studies (focus on death and violence) for EMPoWER – Daphne III. Department of Philosophy, Sociology, Education & Applied Psychology (FISPPA), Section of Applied Psychology, University of Padua (Italy) email: daniela.dilucia@unipd.it

Denise Saint Arnault: Professor at the Division of Acute, Critical, and Long-term Care University of Michigan School, President of Council of Nursing and Anthropology, Chairperson, Research Committee, Michigan State University, expert on Clinical Ethnographic intervention to promote help seeking for East Asian Immigrant Women, email: starnaul@umich.edu

Elisabetta Camussi: Professor of Social Psychology, Department of Psychology, University of Milano-Bicocca, Italy; expert of Feminist research e feminist action research, director of GDG research group; email: elisabetta.camussi@unimib.it

Gabriela Dima: Psychoterapist and teacher of Romanian Association of Classical Psychodrama. Associate lecturer at Transilvania University, Brasov, Romania. E-mail: ela.dima@yahoo.com

Valentina Grosso Gonçalves: PhD, Post-doctoral researcher University of Milan, Bicocca, email: v.grossogoncalves@campus.unimib.it

Angelika Groterath: Professor of Social psychology and Social pedagogy, University of Darmstadt; Director Moreno Institute Stuttgart, DAGG, expert in peace-keeping processes, email: angelika.groterath@h-da.de

Maria Silvia Guglielmin: Psychologist, Psychodramatist, Coordinator Research for EMPoWER – Daphne III; Department of Philosophy, Sociology, Education & Applied Psychology (FISPPA), Section of Applied Psychology, University of Padua (Italy), Director of Psychodrama Theatre in Treviso, email: mariasilvia.guglielmin@gmail.com

Gabriela Moita: PhD, psychologist, psychodramatist. Co-President of FEPTO (fepto.eu), President of the Portuguese Society of Psychodrama; email: np59xi@mail.telepac.pt

Mary Molloy: Psychologist and Professor at Boyesen International Institute of Biodynamic Psychology and Psychotherapy, London; email: mm@biodynamic.org

Marco Monzani: professor of Criminology at the Faculty of Medicine, University of Ferrara, Italy. Professor of Forensic Psychology and Advanced Criminology degree in Psychology at the University Institute of Venice IUSVE, email: mnzmrc@unife.it

Adele Nunziante Cesàro: Full Professor of Clinical Psychology at University of Naples "Federico II"; member of the Regional (Campania) board of the National Association of Psychologists; of the SIUEERPP of Paris, email: adele.nunziantecesaro@unina.it

Sharon O'Halloran: Psychologist and professor at the Department of Mediation, FGBII, SAFE Ireland, email: sharon@safeireland.ie

Leandra Perrotta: Psychologist, Jungian psychodrama trainer and dance-therapist in Turin, Italy; co-president of FEPTO — Federation of European Psychodrama Training Organizations. Contract Professor at University of Valle D'Aosta, email: psicodramma@gmail.com

Ingrid Pogliani: Psychologist, Research & Editorial Research for EMPoWER – Daphne III. Department of Philosophy, Sociology, Education & Applied Psychology (FISPPA), Section of Applied Psychology, University of Padua (Italy), email: ingrid.pogliani@poste.it

Lucia Ronconi: Statistical Consultant and Analyst, University of Padua, email: l.ronconi@unipd.it

Giuseppe Stanziano: Psychologist, Master degree in philosophy, PhD in Gender Studies – University of Naples Federico II, email: giuseppe.stanziano@unina.it

Galabina Tarashoeva: Psychiatrist, psychodrama psychotherapist, manager of Mental Health Center prof. N. Shipkovensk, Director of Psychodrama Center Orpheus, Sofia, Bulgaria. E-mail: orpheuspsychodrama@gmail.com

Ines Testoni: Professor of Social Psychology and Director of Master "Death Studies & The end of life" Department of Philosophy, Sociology, Education & Applied Psychology (FISPPA), Section of Applied Psychology University of Padova, Scientific director of EMPoWER – Daphne III; email: ines.testoni@unipd.it

Claudio Tugnoli: Professor of Moral Philosophy, University of Trento, expert in peace-keeping processes, email: tugnoli53@virgilio.it

Sibylla Verdi: Editorial Associate, Department of Philosophy, Sociology, Education & Applied Psychology (FISPPA), Section of Applied Psychology, University of Padua (Italy) for EMPoWER – Daphne III, email: sibylla.verdi@gmail.com

Michael Wieser: Professor of Psychology at Alpen-Adria-Universitaet Klagenfurt/Wien/Graz, Department of Psychology, Austria, psychotherapist (psychodrama), and Professor in psychodrama training program of Austrian Association of Group therapy and Group dynamics, email: michael.wieser@aau.at

Luigi Zoja: IAAP International Association for Analytical Psychology; AGAP Association of Graduate Analytical Psychologists; CIPA *Centro Italiano di Psicologia Analitica*; NYAAP New York Association for Analytical Psychology; SgfAP Schweizerische Gesellschaft für Analytische Psychologie; mail: luigizoja@fastwebnet.it

Index

A Social Work Journal
Transnational Social Review

The journal "Transnational Social Review - A Social Work Journal" (TSR) offers an international forum to discuss social work and related disciplines and professions from a transnational perspective.
It responds to the challenges of the increasing impact of transnational developments and structures upon social work and related fields.

www.budrich journals.com gives you online access to the content of all journals and periodicals published by both Budrich Publishing Houses.

Verlag Barbara Budrich •
Barbara Budrich Publishers
Stauffenbergstr. 7. D-51379 Leverkusen Opladen
Tel +49 (0)2171.344.594 • Fax +49 (0)2171.344.693 •
info@budrich.de

www.budrich-journals.com